'The devastating impact on the future wellbeing and life chances of a young person, and the choice we have to liberate those affected, is admirably demonstrated through the voice of those who have experienced the effects of bullying and triumphed. I hope this gives pause for thought, renewed commitment, as well as hope.'

– *The Rt Hon David Blunkett MP, former Secretary of State for Education and Employment*

'The eight case studies of bullying in this book are compelling reading. In their own words, young people describe their intense suffering, but also the help they got through Red Balloon. The value of these testimonies is deepened by the thoughtful professional commentaries provided. In addition there is useful advice for teachers, parents, and children, and a description of the Red Balloon philosophy which has proved so helpful for bullied children who are failed by the school system. This is an immensely valuable book which shows the reality of very severe bullying but also has a message of hope which it is vital to disseminate.'

– *Peter K. Smith, Head of Unit for School and Family Studies, Goldsmiths, University of London, UK*

'For two decades Carrie Herbert has been in the vanguard of the fight against bullying: not preaching; not devising the well-meaning strategies, charters and initiatives that too often threaten to swamp schools and teachers while achieving little; but working with schools and workplaces and, above all, working with damaged young people to put their lives back together again. And she does.

[*Rising Above Bullying*] desc
intensive care" to rebuild, slov
and self-esteem of a bullied l
same, but too rarely do so. T

because there are none of those. Instead there is honest but uncompromising advice. The book's forthrightness makes it a hard read at times. It also makes it, all the more, a vital and powerful one.'

– *Bernard Trafford, Headmaster, Royal Grammar School, Newcastle, UK*

'A timely, important and eye-opening book, which gives teachers access to the thoughts, feelings and experiences of children who have been bullied. As someone who was bullied, and who became a school refuser, this book struck a chord with me – it gives an insight into what school really feels like for a bullied child. The practical advice and guidance will be of great help to all those working in schools.'

– *Sue Cowley, teacher, writer and trainer, and author of* Getting the Buggers to Behave

Rising Above BULLYING

of related interest

Bully Blocking
Six Secrets to Help Children Deal with Teasing and Bullying – Revised Edition
Evelyn M. Field
ISBN 978 1 84310 554 1

Cyberbullying
Activities to Help Children and Teens to Stay Safe in a Texting, Twittering, Social Networking World
Vanessa Rogers
ISBN 978 1 84905 105 7

The Bullies
Understanding Bullies and Bullying
Dennis Lines
ISBN 978 1 84310 578 7

Let's Talk Relationships
Activities for Exploring Love, Sex, Friendship and Family with Young People
Vanessa Rogers
ISBN 978 1 84905 136 1

Helping Children to Cope with Change, Stress and Anxiety
A Photocopiable Activities Book
Deborah M. Plummer
Illusttrated by Alice Harper
ISBN 978 1 84310 960 0

Supporting Traumatized Children and Teenagers
A Guide to Providing Understanding and Help
Atle Dyregrov
ISBN 978 1 84905 034 0

Rising Above BULLYING

From Despair to Recovery

Rosemary Hayes and Carrie Herbert

Foreword by Esther Rantzen
Illustrated by Roxana de Rond

Jessica Kingsley *Publishers*
London and Philadelphia

First published in 2011
by Jessica Kingsley Publishers
116 Pentonville Road
London N1 9JB, UK
and
400 Market Street, Suite 400
Philadelphia, PA 19106, USA

www.jkp.com

Library of Congress Cataloging in Publication Data
Hayes, Rosemary, 1942-
Rising above bullying : from despair to recovery / Rosemary Hayes and Carrie Herbert ; foreword by Esther Rantzen ; illustrated by Roxana de Rond.
p. cm.
ISBN 978-1-84905-123-1 (alk. paper)
1. Bullying. 2. Bullying--Prevention. 3. Bullying in schools--Prevention. 4. Self-esteem in children. I. Herbert, Carrie M. H. II. Title.
BF637.B85H36 2011
371.5'8--dc22

British Library Cataloguing in Publication Data
A CIP catalogue record for this book is available from the British Library

ISBN 978 1 84905 123 1

Printed and bound in Great Britain

CONTENTS

ACKNOWLEDGEMENTS

We gratefully acknowledge the contribution from past and present Red Balloon students and from the staff members of Red Balloon Learner Centres. This book could not have been written without their help.

Foreword

Esther Rantzen

I will never forget nearly 20 years ago taking an agonizing phone call from a mother who had just discovered the dead body of her lovely 16-year-old daughter, Katherine. I remember the pain that drove me to my feet, as I stood in the centre of a busy television office, utterly focused on her voice. She told me that Katherine had been bullied, not with kicks and punches, but with the cruelty children can use against each other, the taunts of 'slag' and 'tart'. One especially cruel game had been to pretend to welcome her into their friendship group, then arrange to meet her that evening, but nobody else turned up so she was left alone on a street corner, feeling utterly isolated. In the end her feeling of self-worth was so low, she felt so hopeless that she took her own life.

At the time there was a myth that bullying could only hurt if bones were broken. Some people claimed it was simply a 'natural part of growing up'. But knowing the cost in young lives, and urged on by Katherine's mother, I ran a TV campaign to alert schools to this lethal danger. For Katherine was not, and tragically is still not, an isolated case. It has been estimated that at least 16 children a year commit suicide because they are being so badly bullied. Last year alone ChildLine received 37,000 calls from bullied children.

Volunteer counsellors often tell me that these calls are some of the most painful they receive, because whatever advice they offer to protect these children, the young people have already tried to follow. These children are suffering so badly, they (and their families in many cases) have used every method they could to alert the school to the problem, but the school is either adamantly in denial or else does not know what to do – what they have tried has made the situation worse.

Which is why the work of the Red Balloon Learner Centres and the stories and advice in this book are so vital to children, schools and families. Denial has never saved a young life. The Red Balloon Centres have saved and transformed so many children's lives that they have now developed a philosophy and methodology from which others can learn.

Bullying extends well beyond the school gates. In some cases young people dare not even leave their own homes to take a bus or go shopping. And yet they have done nothing to deserve this torture. For that is what bullying can become. In the two decades since we told Katherine's story on television, I have met many, many children who have experienced horrible, targeted bullying. There seems to be no explanation why one child is singled out, rather than another. It may just be that a child is too clever, too tall, too sporty, too fat or too thin, for some utterly random reason he or she can become the focus of physical or mental cruelty, often a combination of both. And one of the worst aspects is that, as I have discovered over the years, all too often the school or the youth club give up defeated, and end up by excluding or blaming the bullied children themselves and their families. The Red Balloon teams work with these most serious cases, the children who have actually stopped going to school because they have become so frightened. Some of these children have been out of schools for weeks, months and, in some cases, years.

Bullying can wreck lives, destroying a child's ability to learn. I spoke to one government minister who told me that at his school he had suffered vicious bullying for two years and he had changed from being a hard-working outgoing student to a silent no-hoper who dreaded every moment he spent in the classroom and the playground. He supported the development of the Anti-Bullying Alliance, and

Bullying can wreck lives, destroying a child's ability to learn.

I would love to report that bullying is on the wane. But, sadly, technology has provided yet more new ways for bullies to attack their targets, cyber-bullying, gang-bullying, all seem to be flourishing. It's bad for those who suffer, bad for the perpetrators, bad for teachers and youth workers, bad for society.

Red Balloon Learner Centres, founded by Dr Carrie Herbert, exist to pick up the pieces, to recover the children so that they do not suffer long-term damage. You will see the methods used described in this book, and how very effective they are, with a 95 per cent success rate with those who stay at least six weeks. Their students often move on into full-time education or employment with outstanding results, first class degrees among them. This book contains case histories, vividly recording the impact of the bullying, and the way these young lives have been saved (50% of the young people recovered by Red Balloon have been suicidal – so Red Balloon is literally a life-line).

We live at a time when bullying has all too often been glorified, celebrity chefs are admired for it, game-shows have become notorious for it. We need this book more than ever, we need the advice and support Dr Herbert offers within it, we need Red Balloon Learner Centres in every town and city. Whether you are being bullied, or you know someone who is; whether you run a school or a classroom, or have memories yourself of experiencing bullying, I am sure you will find these pages inspirational. I know you will be moved by the young people's stories and I would like to congratulate them on their courage, in allowing their experiences to be used to help and protect future generations of bullied children and above all to give hope so that victims can rise above bullying.

Esther Rantzen

Patron of Red Balloon

Introduction

Rosemary Hayes

This is a book that aims to highlight the issue of serious bullying and to provide insights into its impact on the lives of children, but also to provide advice based on the pioneering work of the charity Red Balloon, which is dedicated to supporting and educating victims of extreme bullying. It is a book for all those who encounter bullying: for those who are being bullied and their families, for the perpetrators and their families and for teachers and other adults who are in a position of influence. And for the bystanders – those who 'turn a blind eye' thinking it is not their business. We *all* have a shared responsibility to ensure the safety of our children; adults must be proactive in putting a stop to bullying behaviour. This involves doing something if you believe a child is being subjected to unkind and unpleasant treatment. Intervening and saying, 'hello, what's going on here' can often defuse a situation.

The sheer scale of bullying is often not recognized; gang-bullying and cyber-bullying, for example, are both relatively new – and they are escalating.

Rising Above Bullying is intended to make readers aware of the long-term effects of bullying – and this is brought sharply into focus by the first section of the book, comprising stories recounted by young people who have suffered such traumatic bullying that they could no longer cope in mainstream education. These young people have allowed me into their lives and I have been horrified by the stories they have disclosed. Most of us think of bullying as a bit of unpleasant behaviour: a poke or pinch here or there, being called a few names, being ignored. What you will read about here is the traumatic, tortuous, systematic destruction of a young person's self-worth and self-belief.

In compiling this book I interviewed eight young people who had experienced extreme bullying to the extent that they were removed from school and attended a Red Balloon Learner Centre. In order to tell me their experiences, these children have had to return to this trauma, share it with me and relive their pain and fear. For some, the bullying happened a decade ago, for some it was only a few months ago. I am enormously grateful to them all and I hope that their courage in contributing to *Rising Above Bullying* will show readers how destructive bullying can be.

Their stories make uncomfortable reading but they are all based on personal experiences – though, for obvious reasons, all names have been changed – and illustrate just how widespread and diverse bullying is. The damage inflicted can be devastating, so it is crucial that bullied children don't suffer in silence. Overcoming their reluctance to admit to being bullied is the first hurdle. Children need to be able to trust not only the person or organization in whom they confide but also their school and their family to deal with the bullying and to keep on top of it. 'Letting on', 'snitching', 'grassing', can often make things worse if ongoing support from school and home is not forthcoming.

To stop bullying, an holistic approach is needed, so it is important to involve the children who do the bullying. Often, they are as vulnerable as those they bully. Their problems need to be addressed but they need to understand – really understand – the impact their behaviour has on those they target. Getting them to read the stories in this book may be one way of bringing home to them the consequences of their actions.

I have compiled this book in conjunction with Red Balloon founder and chief executive Carrie Herbert and the staff at the Red Balloon Learner Centres in Cambridge, Norwich, Merseyside and

North London, who have given freely of their time, answered my questions and set up interviews. They are in a unique position to provide comfort, counselling and one to one targeted education that begins where the child left off learning. They rebuild confidence and teach useful strategies to help students deal with bullying behaviour.

ABOUT RED BALLOON LEARNER CENTRES

In November 1996 Dr Carrie Herbert, a teacher and educational consultant, received a phone call that was to change her life. It was from the parents of a 13-year-old girl called Harriet who had been so badly bullied at a girls-only boarding school that she had taken an overdose. Her parents were asked to remove her from the school.

For six weeks Harriet stayed at home, then her parents heard that Carrie Herbert ran a school for bullied children in Cambridge. In fact, this was not true. At a lecture in Brighton Carrie had indicated that such a school was necessary but, at the time, it did not exist.

However, when Harriet's parents contacted Carrie and told her of their desperation, she invited them to come and see her and to bring Harriet with them.

When they came, they told Carrie of their confusion and helplessness and of their horror that their daughter had been so carelessly cast adrift. As they talked, Harriet, a slip of a girl, sat white faced and mute, staring at the floor, her body language indicating defeat and misery.

Seeing their plight, Carrie made an instant and momentous decision. She told the family that she would, indeed, start a school. Harriet would be its first pupil and she could 'begin on Monday'.

Within six months Carrie had turned her house into a school, recruited teachers, contacted the local authority who sent her more badly bullied out-of-school children and started the slow process of rebuilding shattered lives.[1] This was the extraordinary birth of

1 At the time of writing, Harriet has a responsible job in London, the overdose she took at the age of 13 long forgotten, but she will never forget that first meeting with Carrie Herbert who, quite simply, turned her life around.

Red Balloon, a charity that runs schools for severely bullied and traumatized secondary school children.

By the time they arrive at a Red Balloon Learner Centre, many of these children have attempted or contemplated suicide. Some are suffering from post-traumatic stress disorder (PTSD) and have flashbacks, insomnia and panic attacks. Some are speechless with fear and all have low self-esteem.

Red Balloon has come a long way since 1996 and several new learner centres are now up and running. Through patience, understanding, encouragement and one to one counselling the dedicated staff have helped many young people regain trust and a sense of self-worth in a place where they are safe and valued. No Red Balloon Learner Centre takes in more than 15 pupils at any one time and the children know that they can stay at the school until they are ready to go back into mainstream education, on to college or into the workplace.

At some time in their lives most people have experienced bullying and know how isolating this can be. It is my hope that the recounting of first hand experiences by bullied children and the advice from those who help them will shed light on this insidious and brutal practice, encourage those experiencing bullying to seek help and give adults – and children – the tools with which to tackle it.

Introduction

Carrie Herbert

Not many books I have come across about bullying are written from the perspective of the children who have been bullied. *Rising Above Bullying* takes the view that unless we understand the pain and misery that bullying causes and the impact that that behaviour has on a person's life we will not be in a position to deal with it effectively.

Many people say unkind, thoughtless and humiliating things to each other. Calling people 'bullies' does not help us get to the crux of the matter. Telling people they are 'victims', a word that disempowers and assumes someone needs to be rescued, is also unhelpful in the recovery process.

Many children are bullied during their school career. This is an unpleasant and unwanted phase but most children get through it, shrug their shoulders and say, 'That's life.' For some children, however, that is not the case. For the children we have at Red Balloon the bullying has been persistent and severe and they have been unable to cope with it. Their despair is heard throughout the stories you will read.

Many people who have used bullying behaviour are totally unaware of the impact that behaviour has had on their target. This book highlights the effects of bullying and takes you directly to the source of the child's pain: the fear, the humiliation, the despair or the isolation.

Teachers are implicated in some of the children's accounts in this book. They didn't listen, they may have even perpetrated the bullying, and they misunderstood the impact the behaviour had on the target. We are only human and with over a thousand children in some schools it is clear that many of the personal issues that beset individual children go unnoticed.

Informal or formal procedures embedded in a school's anti-bullying policy are often too difficult for those suffering from bullying to use. Then to be ignored, not taken seriously or told 'You have asked for it' perpetuates the bullying culture. To be expected to have a 'meeting' with those doing the bullying with a teacher who is unaware of the personal and social implications of the 'apology' makes a situation more miserable, frightening and unbearable.

A SHORT INTRODUCTION TO RED BALLOON LEARNER CENTRES

The first thing to say about Red Balloon is that we are different!

Red Balloon Learner Centres do not resemble schools. Each house is in a former domestic residence, which gives a characteristic non-institutional feel to the place. Red Balloon operates for three terms each year, just like regular schools, and the children arrive each morning by 9.00 am and leave at 3.30 pm, again just like 'normal' schools. But it is here that the similarity ends.

A Red Balloon is like a home, a safe place to be, with rooms for different activities, a community room with sofas, a kitchen where good food is cooked daily by the housekeeper. There is no staff room, no playground and children and staff use the same front door, stairs and loos! Home-cooked food is shared daily round a table at lunchtime, staff and students walk around in slippers or socks, and there may even be a dog to pat. Staff strive to ensure that their Balloon does not sound, feel, smell, look or operate like a school.

A Red Balloon is like a home...there may even be a dog to pat.

There are five conditions under which a child is admitted to a Red Balloon. The first two apply to the centre itself:

1. There is a space; we take only 15 children at Red Balloon at any one time. This may be relaxed in the summer term when children are doing GCSEs and are not attending daily but that is at the discretion of the coordinator and trustees.

2. After the child and parents have been interviewed the staff must feel that they are in a position to help this child move forward. The staff are experts in recovering bullied children, but not necessarily in helping children with severe psychiatric disorders.

The other three conditions apply to the student:

3. The student must want to come and be able to attend regularly.

4. The student must want to learn and make academic progress.

5. The student must agree to behave with respect and consideration at all times.

Students are our first priority

The young people who come to a Red Balloon are our first priority. By the time they arrive they have agreed to three conditions: they want to be here, they want to learn and make academic progress, and they will behave with respect. It is the job of each member of staff to ensure that the children's needs, be they academic, social, physical or emotional, are met.

A first-class service

Red Balloon Learner Centres make a commitment to delivering a first-class service to all their students. Each learner is dealt with individually and differently at both an academic level and at an emotional and social level. In addition, a student showing a particular interest in a topic will be provided with the opportunity to develop that interest with a person who has the necessary skills.

Unconditional positive regard

Each child is given 'unconditional positive regard'. Many of our children have not been taken seriously; their concerns have not been listened to with respect nor have they been given the time and attention they require. They are at a Red Balloon Learner Centre to recover. They need specialist attention of the highest order.

Patience is an important characteristic of our staff. The children may need to try you out, push you to your limit to see if you will bully them, shout, give up on them, use sarcasm, and put them down, because that is their experience. Some think they deserve this treatment because they are worthless. They need to be reassured that they are worth something. End of term reports *always* stress the positive.

Negotiated Curriculum

The education programmes a Red Balloon delivers are tailored to the individual needs of each child and are negotiated with the learner.

- Socially and emotionally they have taken a battering – so their self-esteem needs to be rebuilt, their emotional scars need to be mended and they need to have a better understanding of themselves and others.
- Academically they may have suffered by being out of school for some time (weeks, months and in some cases years) and so need a specialized programme to get them back on an academic track and to learn how to learn and take responsibility for their studies.

The Negotiated Curriculum is covered in more detail later in this book (see pp.183–185).

PART I

The Stories: From Despair to Recovery

Children who come to Red Balloon are damaged. They are severely traumatized and recovering them is a painstaking business. Some react to their trauma by being angry and even violent; some are so withdrawn that they hardly communicate at all; some seek constant attention; few trust themselves, adults or their peers. Every child is different but for most the road to recovery is bumpy; there are many ups and downs, faltering steps forward, slipping back.

The young people who have recounted their experiences are real – and they will be reading this book, so there is no detailed description of any negative behaviour during their time at Red Balloon. This is deliberate. Staff at Red Balloon are in the business of rebuilding self-esteem so to describe these difficult times would be counter-productive. The positive is always stressed in students' achievement records and these are what are quoted from at the end of the stories. A child who has come through a horrible time does not need to be reminded of their past behavioural problems when they may have been confused, suspicious, angry, frightened and their self-esteem at rock bottom. However, in the discussion points that follow each story, some of these difficulties are alluded to in general terms and suggestions given as to how some of the related issues can be addressed.

Each one of these stories describes different ways in which bullying can happen and its devastating consequences.

These children all reached the end of their endurance and most of them felt that suicide was the only way out. They found their way to Red Balloon but, of course, many bullied children slip through the net. Hopefully, these stories will help make all of us aware of the many children enduring bullying at school or staying at home, too terrified to go out. We need to understand their despair and the long-term damage that persistent bullying can cause. Bullying behaviour needs to be taken seriously and it needs addressing.

Obviously, in mainstream education, it is simply not possible to devote the same amount of attention to 'rescuing' a bullied child as happens at Red Balloon. Mainstream schools have neither the time nor the resources to undertake this painstaking task. However, in the 'discussion points' following each story, there is advice to teachers and parents about what they *can* do to help these children – and those who use bullying behaviour towards them – and further and more specific advice is given in the subsequent chapters.

1

Jane's Story

Jane was 25 at the time of the interview.

> 'Every night I would lie in bed and hope that I wouldn't wake up in the morning. I prayed that I would die during the night. I hated myself, everyone at school hated me. I was useless at everything.'

Mum says my asthma started when I was four or five. I had to take drugs for it – steroids – and they made me puff up. Mind you, it wasn't just the drugs. I loved to eat and my mum's a terrific cook! So I was a tubby little girl but I was happy and bouncy and I had friends at school and a lovely family – Mum, Dad and my older brother, David. My best friend was called Katie and we did everything together.

Things started to go wrong when I was about eight and Miss Harker started to teach us English.

I'd never found reading easy but no one had made me feel bad about it before.

We always had to read aloud in front of the whole class. I'd wait for my turn, my tummy tensing up and my mouth dry. When Miss Harker pointed at me I'd scrape back my chair and stand up, my legs wobbly. I'd stare at the passage I had to read but it would go all swimmy and I'd feel my heart thumping against my ribs. It wasn't that I was stupid; I could read OK to Mum or Dad, as long as I took it slowly, but when everyone was looking at me and I had to fill the silence with my voice, I couldn't think properly and I'd stumble over the simplest words.

Miss Harker never actually hit me, but she might just as well. She was always holding something – usually a ruler or a blackboard eraser – and she would shout at me and slam the ruler or eraser – or whatever – down on my desk, only just missing my hand. It made me jump.

She'd listen for a bit as I struggled on, then she'd clap her hands together and raise her eyes to the ceiling.

'Right Jane, let's go back to basics shall we?'

She would write out baby words on the board, words we'd learned when we first started reading and she'd make me sound them out in front of everyone.

C – A – T

'Come on Jane, sound it out for us.'

I'd hang my head and mumble 'cat'.

'Louder, so we can all hear.'

The whole class would start to giggle – and she never stopped them. Even Katie giggled, along with everyone else. I suppose she didn't want to be different.

But once the lesson was over no one taunted me and Katie and I would go out to play as if nothing had happened.

I never told Mum and Dad about Miss Harker. I suppose I thought she was justified in shouting at me and making me feel bad because she was frustrated with me, but looking back, she was the first person to chip away at my confidence.

On the whole, though, I enjoyed school and I coped OK with other lessons. It was just the reading out loud I found so difficult.

For the next three years, nothing changed. Miss Harker still taught us English and I still dreaded every lesson with her but then, at last, I was in my final year and it was time to move to a new school.

Mum and Dad had chosen a school they thought would really suit me and Katie was going there too – although there would be no one else I knew. I was scared about going somewhere new where I'd be in the lowest form again, but Katie would be with me and – best of all – there would be no Miss Harker.

So, although I was nervous, I was excited, too.

But when we turned up at the new school, we discovered that Katie and I had been put in different classes. Mum went to the head-teacher and asked if we could be together but she was told that it was school policy to separate children who knew each other so they could make new friends.

I remember that first day very clearly. I walked across the school-yard, my new shoes squeaking, clutching my school bag to my side and squinting at the piece of paper in my hand that gave directions. I opened a door into a big building and then I walked slowly down a long corridor towards my new classroom. My footsteps sounded very loud. When I found the classroom, I stopped. I remember the door was made of dark wood and there was a little piece of glass slotted in the top. I stared at it, psyching myself up to go in. It was still early and there were no teachers about but there was shouting and laughter coming from the other side of the door. I took a deep breath and then, as quietly as I could, I opened the door and crept inside.

Immediately, all the talking stopped and every single pair of eyes turned to stare at me.

I sat down quickly at an empty desk and, after a few moments, the talking and giggling started again.

No one spoke to me but I was sure they were giggling at me. I felt my cheeks burn. Then came the whispers. Whispers just loud enough for me to hear.

'Oh my God, look at the new girl's hair. It's the colour of shit.'

More giggles.

'What a fat cow.'

At last the teacher arrived and lessons started but, by that time, I was so frozen with fear that I couldn't take anything in.

After what seemed like hours, the bell rang for break. I grabbed my bag and ran out of the room. I didn't know where to go. There were groups of children everywhere, chatting to each other, confident, loud. There was no sign of Katie.

I found a place at the bottom of a winding staircase and stood there munching my crisps. I was desperate for a wee but I couldn't remember where the toilets were and I didn't dare ask.

Suddenly, a piece of paper fluttered down from the stairs above. I looked up and saw a group of children leaning over the stair rail, grinning at me. I smiled up at them. Perhaps they wanted to play with me. Perhaps I was being paranoid. Perhaps they liked me after all!

I bent down and picked up the note.

> *To the fattest girl in the school. We don't like you so get used to being alone.*

I screwed it up and threw it on the floor, and then I ran off. I had no idea where I was going but I had to get away from their laughter.

It was always worst when no teachers were around. As soon as I arrived in the morning, it started. The whole class joined in. They would chuck things at me – not hard things but paper darts and rubbers and things like that. They'd all do it, laughing, until I turned round and ran out of the room. And they'd hurl the insults after me, too, always about my weight. There was one boy who went on and on: 'How much do you weigh, Jane? 500 pounds? Or is it more! Come on, tell us how much you weigh!' And there was a group of three or four girls, too – the

Suddenly, a piece of paper fluttered down from the stairs above.

popular ones – and as soon as they started taunting me all the other girls followed.

'No one likes a fatty, Jane. Why don't you lose some weight?'

At first, I tried to hook up with Katie, but she'd made other friends and she always looked embarrassed when I came up to her. Once I overheard one of her new gang saying, 'Why do you hang around with that fat slag?'

After that I kept away from her.

I had no friends. I sat alone at lunchtime and I was never invited to join in any games at break so I tried to find places where I could hide away. My only comfort was food and I would stuff myself with crisps and chocolate while I crouched in my lonely corner. Even then, I wasn't free from the name-calling.

'Look at Jane, stuffing her face again. What a fat slob.'

And they'd all turn and look at me.

Everyone seemed to put me down, not just the children but the teachers, too. Once I won an art competition. I was so proud. I took the painting in to show to my class teacher, but she didn't say much. And as soon as she'd left, the other children all turned on me.

'Not just a fatty, Jane. You're a cheat, too!'

'You didn't do that yourself, did you? You're no good at anything. I bet you got your mum to do it and pretended it was yours.'

At home, Mum knew that something was wrong. I'd cry every Sunday night, I complained of stomach aches, headaches, feeling sick. Anything to avoid going to school.

At last I told her about the bullying.

She went to see the head-teacher but he wouldn't believe her. He said there was no bullying in his school.

So I struggled on for another term but, if anything, the name-calling and ostracizing got worse. I ate more and more to console myself and I began to believe what they said about me. I was just a fat slug who was good at nothing and everyone hated me.

Finally, Mum and Dad couldn't bear seeing me so unhappy so they took me away from that school and I was sent to another school that was supposed to be really caring.

I suppose, when I started there, I half-expected to be bullied – and, of course, I was. I did make one friend but she would only be nice to me if we were alone together. In a crowd she would pick on me, just like the rest.

I still found reading out loud difficult and I could feel the class holding back their laughter as I struggled with the words.

On the whole, the boys at the new school just ignored me. The girls were the worst, specially the pretty, popular ones. They all seemed to be slim with long blonde hair, good at sport and fancied by the boys.

At my first PE lesson I forgot my games kit. As I went into the changing room, three of the girls were there, already changed, looking stunning in their shorts and shirts. One of them, Julie, turned to me:

'Where's your kit, Jane?'

I hung my head. 'I've forgotten it.'

'Well, you'll have to get a PE kit from *somewhere*. Otherwise the teacher will make you do it in your underwear!'

They all started laughing.

'Gross!' said one. 'Think of Jane in her *underwear*! Yuk!'

I wanted to cry. 'What shall I do?' I whispered.

'I dunno,' said Julie. 'You'd better ask the teacher.'

When the PE teacher arrived she sent me to the matron. I got lost trying to find the matron's room and I was too scared to ask the way.

Eventually I found it and the matron gave me some secondhand kit and I made my way back to the gym. I struggled into the tightly fitting clothes and joined the others.

Gym mats, a horse, bars, boxes high and low, benches, climbing ropes.

My worst nightmare.

A whistle blew and we all had to make our way to a section. I went to the easiest, the mats. We were supposed to jump off a springboard, do a somersault in the air and land on our feet, and then do a roll on the mat.

I stood at the back of the line, watching. Everyone else found it easy but I knew there was no way I could do it.

I went up to the teacher. 'Please miss, I can't do that.'

She looked at me as if noticing my blubber for the first time.

'Have a try,' she said.

I lumbered onto the springboard but because of my weight there was hardly any elevation and I fell headlong onto the mat.

Julie and her friends giggled.

'Quiet,' said the teacher. Then she turned to me and sighed. 'Just do a roll on the mat Jane.'

I found this hard enough but I did my best. When I'd finished, I stood up and then limped back to the line of girls. By this time I was biting my lip, trying to hold back the tears.

Julie glanced at me with dead eyes and then she flicked back her hair and went on whispering with her friends.

She looked at me again and there was a little smile on her face. She knew I was a loser – and she knew I was scared of her.

Months later, every day had become a living nightmare. Second after second, minute after minute, hour after hour, day after day, things got worse. Terrifying, threatening notes, whispers and sniggers, death glares.

I've kept some of the notes:

> *Jane, you're so fat. You need to lose weight, but I expect you know that.*
>
> *You have to lose weight. The floor can't hold you any longer.*
>
> *To the fattest girl in the school. If you don't lose weight you're going to die and THAT'S a promise!*
>
> *You're TOO FAT for school. NO ONE likes fat people.*

There was only one week at that school when I wasn't miserable and frightened. I had opted out of a school trip and all my tormenters were away. I still had to come into school and activities were arranged for the few of us left behind. It was quiet, there was no reading aloud, no gym and the others were nice to me.

But as soon as the week was over, it all began again.

It was about this time that I discovered Sophie. I don't know where she came from. She was a person in my imagination. She was everything I would never be – clever, assertive, sure of herself – and I would pretend that I wasn't Jane, I was really Sophie. I used to fantasize about all the things she did. She was a doctor and had her own plane. She flew off to Africa and saved hundreds of children from starvation.

One day, at a family party, I told my auntie about Sophie and she encouraged me to act out being her.

So I found some goggles and a cap and a coat belonging to my dad and suddenly I *became* Sophie. At the party, I marched in, head held high, my voice strong and told everyone what I'd been doing.

'Hello everyone. My name's Sophie. I've just flown in from Africa. Hell of a flight. Had an emergency landing on a tropical island, only just got out alive. Good to see you. Must dash – you know, lives to save, journeys to make. Goodbye.'

All my relations were astonished. Jane, this silent miserable, fat girl was, for a few moments, this other person: a strong self-assured young woman. A flash, perhaps, of what might have been.

For a while, being Sophie in my imagination kept me sane.

But things were getting really bad at school and I felt sick every morning as we approached the school gates. I remember that the song 'Search for the Hero inside Yourself' was always on the car radio, but however hard I searched I could never find my inner hero. In front of others, I could only be that other self – Sophie – if I was dressed for the part.

I started having terrifying nightmares, dreaming that children at school were chasing me, threatening me with weapons and gaining on me. They'd be right on me, brandishing clubs and knives and guns while I tried to shield myself from them.

I'd wake up sweating with fear, my heart pounding.

I didn't know what to do or where to turn.

Every night I would lie in bed and hope that I wouldn't wake up in the morning. I prayed that I would die during the night. I hated myself, everyone at school hated me. I was useless at everything.

Dying was the only way out.

Mum went to the head-teacher to tell him I was being bullied but just like at the first school, he didn't believe her. She went again, this time with my auntie, but still he was adamant that I was making it up.

And it was then that my parents decided to have me taught at home.

The relief when they told me this.

'You mean not go to school again?'

'No, love,' they said. 'We'll get in tutors to teach you here at home where you are safe.'

Safe.

I flung my arms round Mum's neck and burst into tears. That night, for the first time in months, I slept properly.

It was a happy year. The tutors were all lovely and I enjoyed my lessons. I had a strict timetable and one of the rooms in the house was made into my schoolroom. After my lessons, I did cooking with Mum or she would take me on walks and we'd identify flowers and trees.

It was then that I began dieting and Mum helped me. She'd take me to the leisure centre to swim and work out. It gave me such a buzz when the weight started coming off that I began to obsess about it. I took laxatives and I sicked up my meals. I know it was stupid, but I couldn't stop. I was so desperate to get thin.

Thin people are popular.

I made some real friends at the leisure centre, too. They didn't know anything about my past; they just accepted me for myself. And they are still my friends today.

And then the Red Balloon Learner Centre opened. It was specially for people like me who had been bullied and I became one of its first students.

The moment I arrived at Red Balloon I felt safe. Everyone encouraged me and praised me when I made an effort and at last I found myself able to read aloud in front of others. Just knowing that all the students at the school had been bullied was very comforting. I discovered I was good at drama (being someone else made me leave my insecure self behind, just as when I'd pretended I was Sophie).

I stayed at Red Balloon for two years, gradually getting more confident, able to mix with others and contribute to Circle Time and discussions. I often recognized my old self in the new pupils who arrived, miserable and terrified. We always talked through any worries as a group, and we all felt valued.

At Red Balloon I learned to hold my head up high and at last I felt ready to go back to mainstream education.

COMMENTS FROM RED BALLOON STAFF

Jane left Red Balloon and went to Sixth Form College where she passed three A levels and had an offer of a place at university. Before embarking on further study she decided to take a gap year and on her return joined the police force. She now works as a surveillance officer with a national brief.

Jane was a young woman who affirmed you. She was always interested in other people and sensitive to their needs. She was one of life's givers.

DISCUSSION

Carrie Herbert

Bullying because of a person's weight

The bullying that Jane experienced because she was overweight clearly demonstrates that some children are not helped to change the conditions that lead them to be bullied and are not listened to, nor are they supported appropriately.

Overweight people are often bullied. In our society, being overweight equates, in our view, to being unattractive, slothful and lazy. However, a few hundred years ago it was the opposite. Fat people (especially women) were celebrated and in demand. They were admired for being wealthy (having access to plenty of food) and healthy.

People who overeat often do so because they are unhappy. But are they bullied and then eat because they are unhappy – so become fat – or are they unhappy for other reasons, overeat, get fat and are then bullied? An interesting conundrum.

Parents and carers also bear responsibility. An overweight child is presumably the product of parents (or carers) who give a child too much food, too much sugar and fat and do not encourage exercise. The impact of this on the child is in some respects beyond their control. They do not buy the food, cook it or dish it up.

WHAT WE DO AT RED BALLOON

We have also had children who have eating disorders at the other end of the spectrum, anorexia or bulimia. In some cases these conditions arise out of being overweight when the young person, in a desire to lose weight, goes too far. To some extent the story of Emma's treatment (see below) is one which has worked with both 'anorexic' and 'bulimic' students. I use inverted commas as most of the children have not been diagnosed with either condition but arrive saying they have one or other. No pressure is put on them to eat or not eat, a healthy lunch is provided, accommodation is made for individual needs whether that be in the form of food or in the form of another room and often within a few weeks the children resume a healthy eating pattern.

One student, Emma, arrived with a swallowing disorder. She had a lump or restriction in her throat making it impossible for her to eat anything other than soup. This was accommodated at lunchtime and Emma was given a bowl of soup. However, it was pleasing to see that after a couple of weeks her anxiety and fear was reduced to such an extent that she began to eat normally with the other children, giving up soup and taking up sandwiches and baked potatoes.

Whilst we believe that providing a balanced healthy diet is an essential part of the recovery programme there is more to the lunchtime break than just food. Many of our children feared lunchtimes at their previous schools. This was because they found them scary places with little discipline, poor behaviour and a lack of supervision. Many of the children we have at Red Balloon refused to go to their school canteen.

So part of our lunchtime regime is providing a safe and comfortable place in which to eat. Lunchtimes are important times to learn to socialize: manners are taught and employed, boundaries are set and maintained, topics of conversation are introduced and scrutinized and behaviour is monitored. Whilst this may sound tough it means that each child knows that things cannot get out of control, no 'balls from left field will be played', no unkind, unpleasant or intimidating behaviour will happen. It is in this environment that children can continue to recover.

In addition to the behaviour and atmosphere at lunchtime all the food provided is homemade from local suppliers and is seasonal. The housekeeper reduces salt, sugar and fat from the lunchtime meals and the snacks provided. Bread is often homemade as are the soups and other dishes and alongside these meals there is fresh fruit and salad.

Physical exercise for children who have been bullied is often traumatic. In the school changing room, whilst undressing or having a shower, bullying is often exacerbated.

In the following exchange, you can hear Jane's embarrassment and how the uncomprehending, oblivious and ignorant comments made by the teacher only make matters worse.

> I went up to the teacher. 'Please miss, I can't do that.'
>
> She looked at me as if noticing my blubber for the first time.
>
> 'Have a try,' she said.

Red Balloon provides one to one physical activity with a member of staff. This could be in the gym, or on the squash or tennis courts. Sometimes team games are played but these are negotiated and children who find this difficult are excused from joining in.

WHAT TEACHERS AND PARENTS/CARERS CAN DO

As with most topics under the microscope in this book, the main way of dealing with any of these issues is to discuss them openly and constructively, taking into account the young person's views as well as educating them in alternative values or ways of behaving.

Mealtimes can be battlegrounds: they can be extremely uncomfortable occasions; eating can be an embarrassing, awkward event; food can be strange, exotic or boring; knives and forks difficult to wield if unfamiliar. All of these things can contribute to a child not wanting to eat. Stack on top of this a hurried, noisy, challenging break in the school day where lining up, having to handle trays, cutlery, water, unappetizing food, difficult table companions in a school canteen, and there is no wonder that for some children lunch becomes a nightmare.

Eating habits start young. Apparently babies being introduced to food for the first time take approximately three tastes of some new food to like it. By the time that child is a teenager it is 16 tastes. So providing your baby and young child with a varied introduction to food will of course help their taste buds to develop and their confidence in food to grow as they experiment with new and different food textures, taste, colours and combinations.

The ambience of course can have a deleterious effect on whether a child wants to eat and where they choose to eat. Eating alone, grabbing food and running, 'grazing' from the fridge standing up, or eating biscuits from the cookie jar as opposed to eating *en famille* is learned behaviour. A mealtime where the focus is on enjoying food together as well as sharing information about the day makes a time that is enjoyable rather than fraught.

Creating a safe, pleasant, unhurried atmosphere in the lunch hall at school may be difficult when attempting to feed over a thousand children, but not providing this contributes to the problem that young people have eating healthily during the school day.

At Red Balloon we have also had a student who was not able to use a knife and fork with confidence. The handicap of being unable to effectively control food from plate to mouth inhibits children's pleasure in eating.

Reading with confidence

WHAT WE DO AT RED BALLOON

For many Red Balloon children, reading out loud, speaking publicly or reading at an assembly have been times when they have felt at their most vulnerable. We take the view that speaking publicly is a skill that they may well need in future – giving a presentation at work, for example, or speaking at a family celebration. So we help them prepare.

It is strange that adults are rarely asked to read out loud without preparation and it seems unfair that children should be expected to do so, particularly when reading a piece with difficult sentence constructions and unfamiliar words to an unreceptive audience. We ask students to prepare what they want to read aloud, we take time to practise it with them and then prepare the audience to listen positively. Within these parameters, Jane was able to read out loud with fluency.

Children at Red Balloon are encouraged to speak publicly every six weeks or so. At the end of each half term every student is expected to prepare a talk or give a demonstration in front of the other students and the staff, about a piece of work with which they are pleased. These presentations are a feature of Red Balloon life and although many children find them daunting at first, they do much to build self-confidence since the 'audience' is trained to ask positive and encouraging questions and to clap after every presentation. It is very satisfying to see the way in which different children feel relief and joy at the positive feedback they receive.

WHAT TEACHERS AND PARENTS/CARERS CAN DO

Reading out loud, unfortunately, is still an activity that some teachers in primary schools believe to be an essential part of the school day. And although it is a skill that is required and useful for adult life, for some children this activity can put them off reading out loud for many years – in fact can put them off reading at all.

Reading should never be asked of a child who is a beginner, who is reluctant, who is unsure of their ability, as reading out loud is one of the few activities, like singing, which reach right to the core of one's confidence.

Speaking with your child's teacher is one way of tackling this problem, although in the case of Jane this actually made it worse. The teacher, when asked by Jane's mother to allow Jane to skip reading out loud, first made a point of announcing that Jane would not be asked to read but then at the end of the lesson giving every child who had read out loud a house point!

Being a skillful, confident, articulate reader will of course help children with many other skills. Reading at home can help a child with their confidence, so finding out as a parent which reading method is being taught to your child so that you can support it, having a wide range of books at all levels for your child to look at, browse through and read as they grow up is of course the best way to ensure your child will be confident in the classroom when asked to read.

As a teacher, I would never ask a child to read in class out loud unless they had been given time to look through what it was they were to read, ask for help on any difficult or unknown word and had the chance to practise it to themselves. Reading around the class is not a useful activity to my mind; it hinders the flow of the story as each child stops and a new one starts, it shows up those children who are not confident and it ruins the storyline for most of the others.

Using drama in the recovery process

WHAT WE DO AT RED BALLOON

We use drama to help children learn new ways of operating, especially in the face of unwanted or unpleasant comments. Role-play is one of the ways in which we do this and is an essential part of the recovery process. Teaching children how to deal with bullying (using the strategies mentioned later) can be reinforced by acting out a situation.

Within drama there is also the opportunity to become another person. By encouraging Jane to be someone else, and adopt a self-confident posture, she could extrapolate from the role-play and utilize some of the lessons learnt in the real world. Working with Jane on her self-image and teaching her to stand tall, look people in the eye, use 'broken record' (this is a strategy we often use which is explained on p.168) or walk away from situations, provided her with real life skills.

WHAT TEACHERS CAN DO

Drama is a useful tool in schools to help children experience 'being in someone else's shoes'. Whether it is a whole-class improvisation, small-group improvisation, making up a short play, or demonstrating an incident of bullying at a school assembly, there are many ways in which children can experience what it might feel like to be ostracized, taunted, ignored or humiliated.

The issue of bullying can be introduced as a topic for discovery and exploration – especially the feelings that surround those of the child being bullied. Choosing a student to be the one being bullied is a task that should be undertaken with care. The teacher needs to know the student well and make sure that they are happy with that role. Choosing a strong, assertive student is essential. Checking as the improvisation develops is also important. Debriefing at the end of the session is essential so that the children know to leave the feelings aroused during the improvisation in the drama room.

Drama helps children work out alternative and more reasoned endings too. Taking the topic of bullying and asking the children to make up a play about how it started, what happened, what are the feelings of the 'victim', the person doing the bullying, the bystanders and how the bullying can be resolved productively, all contribute to helping all children understand the tensions, the dynamics and the difficulty of dealing with a real incident.

2

Tom's Story

Tom was 13 at the time of the interview.

> 'They never did anything to me where there were cameras. But there aren't any cameras in the toilets. That's where some of the worst things happened.'

Things were OK at primary school until I was ten – in Year 6. I was small for my age – and cocky. Perhaps a bit too cocky for my own good. I've always been able to turn round and make a joke or talk back if anyone badmouths me.

But I really struggled with my reading and writing at primary school. I've got dyslexia and other learning problems – but no one really helped me with this. The head-teacher tried bribing me with sweets, but of course that didn't work. When a word doesn't make sense to you, all the sweets in the world aren't going to make you understand it!

I felt bad about my reading and writing and I didn't like being shown up in lessons. Why did everyone else seem to find it easy when I found it so hard?

'OK, Tom, let's hear you read.'

My head would go numb and the words would swim in front of my eyes.

So a lot of the time in lessons I'd sort of switch off and think of other things.

Maybe I wasn't so quick at the reading and writing but I was pretty quick on my feet and quick with answering back if someone annoyed me.

That's what first got me into real trouble – when I was in Year 6.

There was this boy in my form called Matt Evans. We'd never really got on. He was a big lumbering boy – almost twice my size – and when he badmouthed me, called me names, I badmouthed him right back.

Then one day he went for me. I can't even remember what we were fighting about. Usually I'd race away if he came for me – I could always outrun him – but this time I tried another tactic.

'OK you great ape, come and get me then!'

He hated being called big or fat and I knew he'd take up the challenge. Probably he couldn't believe his luck. This little skinny boy taking him on. He was mad as hell but I expect he thought he'd be able to crush me like an insect.

I watched as he approached. I was taking a risk not running away, but I'd had enough of his insults. This time I stood my ground.

'Come on then, fatty,' I taunted him. 'I'm not scared of you.'

I was pretty scared, but I watched him carefully and just as he was making a lunge for me I stuck out my foot.

He wasn't expecting it and he tripped over and fell flat on his face in the schoolyard.

Well! I didn't feel at all sorry for him and I couldn't hide a grin, but everyone else was making a hell of a fuss – including him. He was yelling and screaming and blubbering all over the place!

He'd fallen heavily and he was a bit bruised and he'd sprained his ankle, but you would have thought I'd murdered him!

The teachers came running up, of course, and all Matt's friends gathered round.

'He tripped Matt up,' they said, pointing at me. 'It was all Tom's fault. He started it.'

'No I did not!' I yelled back. 'He was coming for me. You saw him! He's twice my size. What was I supposed to do?'

'Tom started it. Tom started it. It's all his fault.'

Matt's mates went on and on. I couldn't believe it.

The teachers were really angry with me.

'Look what you've done, Tom! He's badly hurt.'

Nothing to what he'd have done to me if he'd caught me. I would have been pulverized!

It was really mean. No one took my side. No one bothered to listen to my point of view.

I was sent to the head-teacher then and my mum had to come into school, too.

The head-teacher was furious.

'I won't tolerate this behaviour in my school,' he yelled.

I tried to tell him what had happened, but he just wouldn't listen.

'Tom's not a bad boy,' my mum began, but the head-teacher cut her short.

I did a bit of shouting and screaming then. I'd had enough of everyone getting at me as if everything was *my* fault. When I'd finished, run out of steam, the head said, 'You have deliberately injured another pupil, Tom,' he said. 'Your action was inexcusable and I have a good mind to expel you from this school.'

It was a pretty stupid thing to say. I was in Year 6 and it was nearly the end of term anyway.

So I left primary school under a bit of a cloud – and it was all so unfair.

Matt Evans never forgot that I'd beaten him in that fight. He made it plain that he was going to get back at me somehow. He became my arch-enemy. I knew he was going to the same secondary school as me so I was sort of expecting trouble.

The first day at the new school, I walked through the school gates with my stomach in knots, dreading seeing Matt. I spotted him right away and he seemed to have grown a foot taller in the holidays!

He looked at me and scowled. I knew I was in for a bad time. It was a big secondary school but he was in my form. How unlucky was that?

But to begin with it wasn't as bad as I'd expected. He didn't have his old group of friends with him and, like all of us, he was finding his feet at big school. I even tried to make friends with him and for a while we had a sort of truce and I relaxed my guard against him.

I should have known better. He was never going to forgive me for beating him in that fight in Year 6 and he wanted revenge. He was just waiting until he'd got confident again and found some new friends.

About halfway through Year 7 he teamed up with some new mates and formed a gang and that's when he really got started on me. Because he was big, all the members of his gang respected him (they were probably scared of what he could do to them if they didn't!) and because he hated me, they all hated me. They just did what he told them to do.

Although there were security cameras all over the place, Matt and his 'team' (he always called them his team) were clever. They never did anything to me where there were cameras. But there aren't any cameras in the toilets. That's where some of the worst things happened.

I'd try not to go near the toilets if I could help it, but there are times when you've just got to go!

One of Matt's team was always watching me, seeing what I was doing, where I was going and however careful I was, they'd spot me and follow me.

They never did anything to me when there were cameras. But there aren't any cameras in the toilets. That's where some of the worst things happened.

I'd rush in, my stomach churning, and do my business, but then they'd be there, waiting for me. They'd sneaked into the toilets behind me.

'Look who's here! It's little Tommy!'

'Thought we couldn't see you, didn't you.'

They'd surround me.

Usually I was punched and kicked. They'd all attack me at once.

One time, one of the gang had a really sharp pencil and they stabbed me with it. Not just a little prod but really vicious hard stabs and they only stopped when I started screaming.

I looked down at this open wound on my leg that was pouring blood. I couldn't stop the bleeding so I went to the first aider and told her what had happened. 'They attacked me in the toilets,' I said. 'They had this sharp pencil and they kept jabbing me with it.'

But she didn't take it seriously. She just gave me an ice pack to put on my leg and told me it would be OK. I remember sitting through the next lesson, the ice pack stinging like hell and blood still trickling down my leg.

I had friends at secondary school. Good friends who always supported me. One – Josh – would step in to help me, no matter what. And he sometimes got attacked for helping me. And there was Luke who always sat next to me – but he wasn't as physically tough as Josh. But he used to try and distract the bullies when they were getting at me. And a girl, Tara, was my friend, too, but she wasn't tough and she stayed out of arguments.

None of my friends were as big or as tough as Matt Evans and there weren't as many of us.

It was often bad at lunchtime and that's where my nippiness helped me. I could always outrun Matt and his team and also I was really good at climbing trees. There was this big tree in the yard. When the name-calling and stuff got bad I would get away from them and take my lunch up the tree to eat it.

Matt was too heavy and clumsy to come up after me.

It was against the rules but I didn't care. It was peaceful up there and I didn't have to watch my back all the time. Sometimes one of my friends would join me in the tree while Matt and his followers would sit at the bottom. They reminded me of a pack of animals waiting for their prey.

They would settle down at the bottom of the tree and yell insults up at me. I'd hear the taunts drifting up towards me.

'Skinny little runt!'

'Tom can't even read!'

'Baby!'

I tried to ignore them but it was difficult and little by little, it really got to me. It wore me down. Why didn't they pick on someone else? Why was I *always* their target?

Matt's gang members were weak. Individually they were powerless and sometimes, using my wits, I could get them to turn on each other. And even on him. But that didn't get me anywhere and it just made Matt all the more determined to make my life as bad as he could.

The tree was one safe place to be and another good place to go was the library. I knew I'd always be safe there because my friend's mum worked in the library and she always looked out for me. They couldn't get at me there and I could breathe easily for a while.

Luckily they never managed to get my mobile number, otherwise I know they would have sent me threatening texts and calls. That would have been really bad. At least I was rid of them when I went home in the evening. If they'd got my phone number I would have been a target 24/7.

They tried accessing my Facebook, too, but I found a way to block them. I've got about 150 friends on Facebook.

Even though the school website said that the school had a no bullying policy, if they did have an anti-bullying policy, then it certainly didn't work. The teachers at the school *never* dealt with the bullying I experienced there. The staff must have seen what was happening to me – yet they chose to ignore it.

My work was going from bad to worse. The school had been very rough and it was trying to get a better reputation so kids were really under pressure to perform. And I *wanted* to perform. I wanted to get an education so I could have a decent job, but I had real problems with my lessons – and with the teachers and teaching assistants. I nicknamed them the vultures – always picking on me.

It seemed to me that I was always being picked on, not only by Matt and his 'team' but by my teachers, too.

They were always picking on me but never helping me. The Special Needs woman who was supposed to help me was useless. She spent most of our time together moaning about her own life.

By this time I was in a mess. Although I pretended to my friends that I didn't care what Matt and his friends said about me or did to me – said what an idiot he was – deep down I did care and I was scared a lot of the time. It's horrible to go round every day knowing that at the next moment someone might kick you or punch you or say vicious things about you.

You can't relax for a moment – and you can't learn anything when you are scared. Scared and unhappy.

Things came to a head when I lost it with one of my teachers. She was going on and on and on at me about my work being crap. Always the same thing, over and over, again and again.

If my work was such crap why was no one helping me?

No one ever helped me!

Suddenly my head exploded and I yelled and screamed at her.

I don't know what I said. I was so mad and angry that I can't remember. All I know is that, at that moment, I'd reached the end of my rope and I didn't want to stay in the place any longer.

Of course I was sent to the head-teacher but by that time I was past caring. I yelled and screamed at her, too.

'I hate it here! No one helps me. No one listens to me.'

And then I walked out.

I had no idea what would happen to me but just to be free of the crap I was taking at the place was a big relief.

I never went back there as a pupil, though I still take part in the drama group that meets at the school and I see my old friends there. I like acting because I can be someone different and I can express myself without being told off.

The school kept emailing me to get me to return but in the end I told them to leave me alone or I'd go to the press and say what hell I'd had there.

I didn't want to be at home all the time, though, and Mum was really worried about me. I wanted to learn. I didn't want to end up with no qualifications and a dead end job.

It wasn't a great time. I had too much time to myself. Time to think about the mess I was in. And I didn't know how to climb out of the hole and get on with my life.

Then one day I was contacted by the people at Peacock House. Somehow they'd heard about me and wanted to help. My mum thought this might be some sort of scam but I checked it all out. Peacock House is specially for kids like me – it's a temporary place where you can go and be safe. A place of refuge.

Well! When I got there, I thought I'd died and gone to heaven. There was all this great equipment and the place was small and bright and cheerful. They took us on great outings, too, like canoeing and stuff. The staff there really helped me. Although I didn't have much teaching – only a couple of days a week – they set me homework I could do in my own time. And there was a fantastic counsellor. She was the first adult I'd spoken to who really understood. She helped me so much with my reading and writing and I could tell her *anything*. There was nothing I couldn't talk to her about.

But I'd always known it couldn't last. You could only stay there for two terms, max.

Then my psychiatrist told me about Red Balloon and my mum helped me to get in. Having had such a good experience at Peacock House I knew that places existed where I could be safe – and happy – so when I heard that Red Balloon was set up in a house and that there were only a few students and that you could learn at your own pace, I knew I'd be OK there.

I have a lot of help here and my reading and writing's come on. I've made some good friends, too, and I feel safe.

The staff encourage me in all sorts of ways. Not just with school work but with all the other things I like doing. With drama, singing and dancing, playing bass guitar, making podcasts and YouTube videos.

I still go to the drama club which takes place at my old school. I wouldn't give that up for anything. It takes members from all over – not just the school pupils. Sometimes I see Matt or members of his 'team' in the corridor at the school or just hanging about in the street, looking spare. I ignore them. My life's moved on and I don't care about them any longer.

Matt's put on a lot of weight. Now I see him differently and I almost feel sorry for him. I can imagine him in the future, vegging out in front of the TV, stuffing himself with junk food. He's never going to make anything of his life and he'll end up in some dead end job – or on benefits.

But I'm determined to get somewhere. I'll stay at Red Balloon until the end of the summer term and then I'm going to a secondary school close by. It's a big place but I'm confident I'll be OK there – and if I do have any problems I know I can always come and talk to the staff at Red Balloon and get help.

One day I'm going to be a radio DJ. So watch this space!

COMMENTS FROM RED BALLOON STAFF

Tom is an interesting and endearing character with huge energy; he has moments of real splendour.

He played a key role in some of the plays put on at Red Balloon and because he was secure in his ability he was thoughtful and generous to others while involved in these productions. He also enjoyed playing in the band.

Here are extracts from some of his Red Balloon achievement records:

> 'You have a great deal going for you, Tom, and as long as you can persevere and keep that sense of humour working for you, you will succeed in whatever you choose to do in the future.'

> 'You are wonderfully articulate. You are very good at keeping a discussion going...you are witty and sensitive and able to use your imagination to the full.'

> 'You are a good and truthful friend, understanding when someone has a problem.'

And here is what Tom put in his own report just before he left Red Balloon:

> 'This year has been OK, just a couple of problems with home stuff but school has been brill. Band has been a rave. I can spell some words and I can type fast and I know how to paint.'

DISCUSSION

Carrie Herbert

Fear of failure

Many of the children who experience serious bullying have difficulties with the concept of 'failing'. Whether that is failing in the academic subjects, on the sports field or at a card game, the same feelings, emotions and behaviour are often exhibited.

It is interesting to speculate why these children feel so badly when they fail. One answer is that they see themselves as having failed at life. They have no friends, they are 'losers', they have had to leave school, they have let their parents down and now they are unable to go to school so they are failing at their studies too.

One way to cover up mistakes is for a child to refuse to do an activity. Either 'I can't' or 'I don't want to' are clear examples of a child not wanting to attempt in case they fail yet again.

Yet it is sometimes through our failures and our mistakes that the best learning happens. So helping children attempt something new, discussing what might happen if they fail, playing out various scenarios of 'what ifs', makes failure 'explicit', helping them tackle a new problem and make the 'mistake'.

WHAT WE DO AT RED BALLOON

Helping students understand that failing is part of life is one of the ongoing tasks for the teachers and other staff at Red Balloon Learner Centres. The educational philosophy on which Red Balloon is based, Negotiating the Curriculum (which features later in this book pp.183–185), goes some way to helping children take control of their learning and thus take control of their failing. If they choose what they want to study, within a range of topics; if they choose what they will explore and the ground they intend to cover; if they set their targets – an essay, a painting, a film, a board game – then they are also in control of their product. If one goes a step further, as we do at Red Balloon, and encourage the children to decide how something will be evaluated, again we are giving the student the power to decide whether something is a failure or not.

Marking pieces of work without the child being present is a waste of the teachers' time. Working on a piece of writing, maths or art together is a learning opportunity.

Many of our children feel let down and are angry about the way adults in particular have not listened, not taken note and, above all, have failed to do anything about the bullying that they experienced. They are also angry that the child (or children) who was responsible for the bullying is still at school.

Family issues

Of course there are many other things apart from bullying for a child to be angry about. The fact that Dad doesn't live with them; that Grandma died; or that they believe an older/younger sibling is preferred. These fears however are very much part of our growing up anxieties. How many of us remember thinking, 'Am I really the child of my parents or am I adopted?'

At Red Balloon we see many children who are disruptive and fear failing and in the first few months the received wisdom is to listen, to be there, to work with – not against – the child, to help them to do some more listening and to allow the body and the mind to calm down, to stop being defensive, to stop getting angry and to begin to engage the brain in well-thought-out options not irrational defensiveness, slick answers or sarcastic comments.

Many of the children we have at Red Balloon have been badly let down not only by the system but by individuals – teachers, head-teachers, parents or peers.

Rebuilding relationships

Rebuilding relationships between children and adults is a speciality at Red Balloon. This is done slowly and painstakingly. I remember one student we had who had been abandoned by his teachers and who was described by them as being 'lazy, difficult, and unattractive'. For nearly a year he lay on the sofa at one of our centres. In those

12 months he watched, he listened and he worked out how he would be treated if he were to partake in what we offered.

What he saw was one to one relationships, children being allowed to deal with their own pain in their own way, children being treated differently to accommodate their individual needs, specialist food for some children, specialist treatment for others. Once he felt that his differences could be accommodated and his idiosyncrasies accepted he joined in.

Within a few months he had found his confidence and he became the unofficial 'leader' and the chief negotiator for the students.

Individual treatment lies at the heart of what we do. Children who have a special talent in drama, music, languages or sport are encouraged to develop it. Red Balloon will provide specialist teachers if at all possible, be that a Tai Chi expert or a Hebrew teacher. In this way we can demonstrate that each child is worthwhile, special and requires different treatment.

'That is not fair' is not a cry we hear much because the children know that they are allowed, indeed encouraged, to be different and with that comes differentiated handling.

As young people recover at Red Balloon so their behaviour changes. When they first come some are depressed, some are quiet, some are angry, some are frightened, some are brittle and some are bright, defensive chatterboxes as if to deflect any unkind remarks.

Red Balloon has a policy that children are not left alone, are not allowed out alone and that there is always a member of staff around to make sure behaviour is respectful and professional at all times. When behaviour lapses this is pointed out to the student.

As children recover, so does their sense of self-worth and in some cases they begin to challenge the 'intensive care' we offer. 'I want to go out at lunchtime' is met with a realization that this child is recovering well and will soon be able to leave and go back to mainstream school.

Red Balloons are like 'intensive care units' in hospitals. A child arrives broken and battered, with multiple wounds, hurts and damage. Our intensive care includes one to one work at the child's academic level, negotiated learning programmes, personal and social education to understand human nature, therapy to understand what happened and healthy food, space and time.

Once a child has recovered in a hospital bed they want to leave. The same applies to a Red Balloon. Once a child has found his or her feet they want out. They want to have friends, to socialize, to go to the cinema or bowling with a group of their peers. Built into the recovery process is the indominatable human spirit that, once recovered, is curious, eager to become independent and wants no more coddling!

Tom left Red Balloon with far more skills – both educational and emotional – than he had when he arrived. During the time with us he learnt how to compromise, to thank people, to think before he spoke, to consider others' viewpoints and not to blame others for the situations he brought on himself. This awareness of self and others is a key attribute of the Personal and Social Education Programme at Red Balloon.

WHAT TEACHERS AND PARENTS/CARERS CAN DO

Fearing failure is a common problem with many children who feel they have to compete with other students in their class, siblings in their family or other children from their neighbourhood. We live in a time when competition in school – to meet targets, to sit exams successfully, to gain admittance to one school or another – does not help a child who has little self-confidence, feels devalued and when compared with others emerges less favourably.

Work in classes on raising self-esteem and to value diversity is one way of helping individual children recognize that we are not all alike and that difference should be celebrated. In a school setting, Circle Time is an ideal opportunity for children to find out from each other that we all have periods of self-doubt, we all have relationships that sometimes go wrong, we all have parents who are frustrating, and so on. Setting up Circle Time and setting the ground rules in a class are very important. At Red Balloon we have rules of not interrupting, listening attentively, not putting people down, not making facial grimaces that show a negative emotion (such as rolling one's eyes, shaking one's head) and no private talking, such as whispering. By establishing a modus operandi Circle Time can be a weekly session where the children work together, share ideas, fears, concerns and frustrations. Creating a healthy class community where the children are caring, tolerant and supportive will also help their ability to learn effectively.

Some of the questions that the children at Red Balloon like best to address – and they like to hear the answers of the other children too – are questions that deal with the individual, their emotions, their values and their beliefs: 'What frightens you the most?', 'What makes you angry?', 'Where do you feel the safest?', 'What is the funniest experience you have ever had?', 'What is the thing you fear to fail at the most?', 'What would you do if you won a million pounds?' These are questions and answers that are often not addressed or discussed as a class.

Of course setting up a robust structure to make sure that children's contributions are respected, not ridiculed, is a slow process, so asking these revealing questions cannot happen in Circle Time on the first occasion but must only be introduced once a level of engagement has been reached, equal respect demonstrated and group identity established.

So understanding the differences in each other is likely to make us more caring, tolerant and sensitive human beings. This in itself can help children address their feelings of failing, especially if they know there are others in the class with the same feelings.

3

Hailey's Story

Hailey was 14 at the time of the interview.

> 'I would come home covered in bruises and kick marks which really worried Mum.'

The bullying began not long after I started at the village primary school. I was very small for my age and probably a bit shy, but Mum says to begin with I was happy to go to school and looked forward to being with other children.

But once the bullying began I never wanted to go out of the house in the mornings; I would dawdle over my breakfast, putting off leaving as long as possible, and then I'd cling to Mum at the school gates, not wanting her to go and begging her not to leave me.

I didn't make friends easily and I was often left standing on my own in the playground. And being on my own and not surrounded by a group of friends made me an easy target I guess. There was one boy – Nathan – who regularly tormented me. He would thump me and push me around, kick me, slam doors on my face if I was standing behind them and make sure I was always left out of any games he and his friends were playing. I would come home covered in bruises and kick marks which really worried Mum.

Mum went to talk to the school and they said that what was happening to me was just the rough and tumble of the playground. But other kids weren't getting the treatment I was getting! No one else was going home covered in bruises like I was.

To be fair, the head-teacher did try, then, to get a group of girls to accept me and let me join in with their games and stuff, but that's not how it happens, is it? Kids have to *want* you. It's no good trying to force them to accept you.

Not surprisingly, it didn't really work out; I never felt a part of their group and the girls soon drifted away and left me on my own again.

Then one day there was this incident with Nathan that really frightened me.

I've always been quite athletic and good at games and I loved going on all the sports equipment. I don't know whether Nathan was jealous that I was good at all that stuff and didn't like it that a girl was sporty. He certainly had a problem with me and maybe that was part of it. Anyway, one day I was on the climbing frame at playtime and I saw Nathan coming towards me. He yelled at me to get off the climbing frame but I took no notice.

Why should I get off? I was enjoying myself!

I knew I'd made him angry but I never thought he'd attack me the way he did.

He was determined to force me off. He swarmed up the climbing frame until he was close enough to attack me. First he trod on my fingers and then he grabbed me round the throat so hard that I was choking and couldn't breathe; I swear to God he was trying to strangle me.

It was a vicious attack; worse than anything he'd done to me before. I fell off the climbing frame gasping for breath, holding my neck and sobbing.

For a long time after that I would have nightmares about being strangled and I'd wake up trying to push away my strangler. It lived with me for a long time, that attack, and Mum says that I even acted out the strangling on my Action Man.

Poor Action Man! I guess I was pretending he was Nathan!

Mum wrote to the school to tell them about the incident and they promised to look into it. Hard to believe, but apparently none of the teachers had seen it happen!

I was so scared by the attack that I didn't want to go back to school after that but the head-teacher said she'd make sure I was looked after.

Nothing changed though. Nathan just kept on persecuting me and his family joined in, too. The last straw was when his sister spat in my food. That was when Mum took me away from the place.

We had a letter from the school saying they were looking forward to seeing me back but I never went back after that and they never contacted us again.

It was as if I had never existed.

I was out of school for almost a year before I started at a different primary school. You can imagine how difficult I found it, going back to school after a year out!

It was so hard, being left there the first day and I felt really vulnerable, looking round and seeing all these kids who already knew each other, playing happily together. Would they all pick on me? Would they all end up hating me?

I bit my lip and frowned and tried to be invisible.

But despite my fears, to begin with I was happy at the new school and not scared and slowly I began to relax.

Unfortunately my happiness didn't last long. A new boy, Justin, arrived. At first he was OK with me but then things started getting bad when we played football. I loved playing football and I was pretty good at it and, like Nathan at the other school, I don't think Justin liked that so he started teasing me, saying I looked like a boy.

Then gradually he got a group of friends round him – mostly boys – and they all ganged up on me and the teasing turned really nasty and got out of hand. They would call me names like 'Hailey-shit' and push me on to a bench and force me backwards. They all took turns in abusing me, verbally and physically.

'What is it – a boy or a girl?'

'Says she's a girl but she looks like a boy!'

'You're a boy, Hailey-shit, you're a boy!'

'Oddball!'

'Freak!'

All this accompanied by shoving and pushing and poking.

I guess it was around this time that I began to learn to fight back and give as good as I got. And once I got angry at someone I found it very hard to control myself.

That's when my rages started. My anger gave me strength I didn't know I had! I found that I could take revenge on my tormenters.

One time this boy was going on and on at me, so I tripped him up and punched him in the face. He didn't know what had hit him and he was so humiliated that he'd been floored by a girl that he never said anything; he never let on to the teachers or his friends because he didn't want anyone to know!

So things weren't great at the new primary school but by this time I knew that I was strong and could survive. I didn't care what other people thought of me; I was tough and I thought I could cope.

And then I went up to secondary school.

Unfortunately, Justin was also at the secondary school but by this time his behaviour was getting worse and worse and eventually the staff there picked up on this and he was expelled.

For a while, after Justin was expelled, people were nicer to me and didn't give me so much grief but the damage had been done and by then I was constantly angry, and suspicious of others. I didn't realize that part of me was shutting down and that I had become too suspicious to believe anyone liked me or wanted to be my friend.

I attended school and went through the motions. In class the teachers didn't seem to notice me much which was fine by me; as long as people left me alone I didn't get into trouble and my temper didn't flare up. And although I found some of the lessons hard, I was learning OK and I was good at drama and at sport.

But I took offence really quickly. I was a cheeky sod and also when my temper *did* flare I'd lose control. I would shout and swear sometimes in lessons if someone annoyed me and I was always getting into fights outside the classroom; a couple of times I got suspended for this.

I was moved to a different class for a while and things got a lot better. But after half term I was moved back; the teachers said I wasn't coping with the work in the new class. This didn't do much for my self-confidence but, as always, I hid any hurt or humiliation by getting angry.

There were endless meetings with me and Mum and the school staff and at one of these Mum and I were shocked when a teacher yelled at me.

'Teachers shouldn't yell,' I thought. 'That's my speciality!'

I carried my anger home, too, and once I completely trashed my room.

The trouble was that I couldn't handle my own angry feelings and when they erupted I had no control over myself. Mum suggested a system of cards – like at a football match – that I could get out when I felt my temper rising and then I could put a card out on my desk (yellow for warning, red for danger), so that the teacher knew what was happening, and then I could leave the room until I had calmed down.

We raised this at one of the meetings and everyone thought this was a great idea but it was only at the very end of my time at that school – just before the really bad incident – that it was introduced. And by that time it was too late.

That final really bad incident happened in class. I was sitting between two boys, Daniel and a new boy, and they were both being bastards. Every time I turned a page in my book one or other of them would put their pen in the book and stop me turning the page. In the end I grabbed the new boy's pen and flung it across the room. The teacher saw and immediately told me off – *me* not *them* – even though I tried to explain that it wasn't my fault and that the boys had been winding me up.

'It wasn't my *fault*! Didn't you see what they were doing to my book? They were winding me up!'

But no one listened and I was sent to stand outside the classroom.

As I stood there waiting for the lesson to end, my anger mounted. I was really really furious; it was so unfair!

By the time the class broke up I had got myself into a real state and as soon as I saw Daniel coming out into the passage I saw red. I wanted to kill him. I grabbed him and got him in a head lock. I kept yelling at him to say sorry. Then the teacher came up and told me to let go of him.

'No I won't. He's got to say sorry,' I yelled. And I pushed Daniel into the door.

The teacher kept saying 'Let go of him' but I kept refusing. Then another teacher came up to see what was happening and she asked me to let him go but I wouldn't. Then she spouted some stuff about being able to use force to make me release him.

That's when I went ballistic. First I punched Daniel in the stomach and then I went for the second teacher and punched her in the face. Her glasses flew off and I kicked at her as she fell backwards. Then I went for the first teacher. I grabbed her hair and pulled her until she fell over. By this time another teacher had come up and she shouted at me to calm down.

It was then that I ran off down the stairs. I went straight to my form tutor and told him what had happened and, to be fair, he did listen to me as I blurted out my side of the story. 'I just wanted him to say sorry,' I said. 'It was *his* fault, not mine. I wanted to hear him apologize.'

My form tutor heard me out. But then he sent me to the head-teacher.

As I walked into the room I knew, in my heart, what was going to happen. The head-teacher went on and on about my behaviour, how my anger and violence against other pupils and staff was unacceptable. How the school had to protect others and how this time I had gone too far.

They felt they couldn't keep me there any longer so I was expelled.

It's hard when you have no 'stop' button. Everyone gets angry sometimes but when I get angry I turn into this wild person, lashing out and swearing and feeling that everyone is against me.

Although part of me wanted to be left alone, after I was expelled from secondary school I was pretty low. And still angry with everyone and everything. Probably, deep down, I was angry with myself but it was easier to blame others – the school, my mum – anyone but me.

It was a difficult time, being at home on my own with Mum. I had some home schooling but I wasn't really in a fit state to learn anything.

That's when I went ballistic.

My head was in too much of a muddle. I was lonely, too, but I didn't want to see other kids and risk being taunted and made angry again.

It was a dark period that time alone at home. I didn't like myself, I didn't like my mum. And there was always this rage inside me, a rage that made me hit out at things, fling stuff around. Anything to give vent to the frustration I was feeling inside. Frustration that I couldn't learn, couldn't make friends and had no idea what would happen to me next. Where could I go from here?

There were visits from the education authorities and I was sent for assessment to a special clinic. Then one day, a guy they brought in to one of the meetings mentioned Red Balloon to us.

Mum and I were told all about Red Balloon so we decided to go and have a look round the place.

As you can imagine, I was pretty suspicious by then of going to any school but when we got there I was very surprised. It felt more like a home than a school because it is in a normal house and I felt accepted immediately. Being there has really helped me.

The teachers at Red Balloon had faith in me and believed in me. And it was at Red Balloon that I discovered that I could get on with new people better than I thought I could. At my other schools I'd often been late or skipped lessons but at Red Balloon I never once skipped lessons. I still got angry when I was there but it was usually at myself for getting things wrong – I wasn't usually angry with other people. Except once in a game of basketball when this boy was tugging at my T-shirt. He kept on and on doing it and finally I lost it and started yelling at him. But, at Red Balloon, whenever I felt angry, I talked it over with the staff and we dealt with it.

And because I was happier, I did more stuff. I found I could make people laugh and I really enjoyed being in the end of term play. My anger seemed to dissolve at Red Balloon and I could relax, make friends and learn.

Everyone at Red Balloon was really supportive – the staff and the other students.

COMMENTS FROM RED BALLOON STAFF

From the first, Hailey was outgoing, keen to fit in and join in whatever activity was suggested. After she had been with us for only a couple of weeks she took part in a play and when another student put a little make-up on her for the role, Hailey couldn't believe the transformation; couldn't believe she looked so good!

Practical things motivated her – particularly piano, art and sport – and if she set her mind to do something in these areas, she showed considerable determination to carry it through.

She soon made friends with a group of boys where her sporting skills were much admired, and she thoroughly enjoyed outward bound activities.

While she was with us she was a delight to teach, usually happy and motivated, and probably the most liked pupil by her peers.

Here are some extracts from Hailey's achievement records at Red Balloon:

> 'has learnt to think of others'
>
> 'a joy to teach'
>
> 'defuses a tense situation with her humour'
>
> 'joins in class discussion and activities with enthusiasm'
>
> 'You are gutsy and warm, you are direct and full of life. It makes you a powerful and passionate person. You have energy and commitment; you have the courage to stand up for yourself and say honestly what you think and feel; in drama you have risen to the challenge of performing in the group's play and are doing a fantastic job! … you have also taken a role in making some of the props. You are a real star!'
>
> 'I am so impressed by the confidence and friendliness that you have brought to Red Balloon. I have seen how quickly you have developed friendships with the other students.'
>
> 'Doesn't matter what others have told you in the past. And it doesn't matter what others have made you believe. You are a good and lovely person, smart and interesting too. Thank you for making a difference in the Red Balloon Community.'

Hailey thrived at Red Balloon – to such an extent that after less than a year both she and the staff at Red Balloon felt that she had come so far that she should move back into mainstream education.

She often comes to visit us to tell us how she is getting on.

DISCUSSION

Carrie Herbert

Today's young people have additional pressures to those born in previous generations. Today's young people could be forgiven for complaining that their childhood has been eroded, pre-empted and controlled by the media, pop stars and the music makers. The fashion industry also targets young people relentlessly. Branding, logos, accessories, make-up for pre-teens all deluge young people. Multi-channel television, MSM, mobile phones and the film industry have forced children and young people to constantly look at themselves, to measure their achievements, physical appearance and academic prowess alongside their peers and in many cases to find themselves wanting. They are not tall enough, not clever enough, they are too skinny, too fat, too dark haired, not blonde enough and with the wrong coloured eyes.

For some this is overwhelming and it becomes a source of despair and anguish for children and teenagers. Young people want to own the latest gear, phone, branded clothes and have the spending power to go to the cinema, roller skating and cafés with their friends. Of course this has an effect on the family as a whole and in particular for some parents, especially those on their own, on a single wage. Suddenly the relationship between a parent and their child becomes a battlefield as the child wants power and control and the parent wants a quiet life. Friction at home is exacerbated by competition as to what to wear, whether the trainers are the right brand, whether a child can stay out until nine or ten o'clock at night.

Not fitting in

Bullying of course is an issue that affects young people if they see their clothes, their trainers, or their way of life as 'wanting'. Young people can be very cruel about how they describe how other children dress. Recently working with some girls in a private school I was made aware of the way boarders can 'get at' each other. One girl, a very ordinary, sporty, blonde girl whose parents lived abroad was accused of 'looking like a man' and wearing a shirt that looked like '1960s wallpaper'.

Uninterested in clothes, make-up, boys and 'girly pastimes' this 13-year-old found it impossible to get a group of friends around her. She slept in a dormitory with two others – the main offenders.

As the bullying set in so she became more isolated and more angry about her situation. She felt she had no one in the boarding house in whom to confide and I – as the 'outside counsellor' – was the recipient of her misery and grief. Yet she was reluctant to do anything about it. She wanted no one told and no member of staff alerted.

After a few sessions of role-play (I would play one of the children doing the bullying, then her), improvisation (we would re-create the scene and play it out differently), discussions about her feelings and other devices to have the opportunity to look at the situation from another angle, she rang me to tell me that she had dealt with it. 'I told them,' she said triumphantly. Apparently at about 11.00 pm when the lights had been turned out they had begun taunting her. She decided she had had enough and said in a very clear voice. 'You have been treating me like this for the past three months. You have called me names and humiliated me. You have said I am a man. You know I am a girl. It makes me feel angry and upset. I want you to stop.'

There was silence and then one of them said, 'You are right and I am sorry.' The other girl did not respond. By the next morning the bullying stopped.

WHAT TEACHERS AND PARENTS/CARERS CAN DO

It is anodyne to say that all children are different and should be treated as such – but it is true, disregard it at your peril! I have witnessed parents wanting their sons to be strong and tough (boys don't cry) and girls to be pink and dainty. But the fact of the matter is every child has to find their own way and to suppress a child's curiosity with make-up, or desire to wear particular clothes, their predilection to climb trees as a girl and to play with dolls as a boy could lead to a range of behaviours that manifest themselves later in the adolescent years. Some of these behaviours could be anger, violence, guilt, deceitfulness or lack of self-worth.

So it is important for homes and schools alike to 'allow' children to try out different things. Some boys want to try out Mum's make-up, put on high heels and wear a skirt – to see what it feels like. Little boys in the 'Home Corner' at nursery school want to try out at being Mother. Some girls like to look like a boy, play football, jump in puddles and get dirty. They would rather play with the boys in the school playground than play with the girls at skipping. Interestingly as a society we are much more tolerant of girls being 'tomboys' than boys being 'girls' – in fact we don't even have a word for it that is neutral!

However letting children experiment with a whole range of different clothes, behaviours or toys will give them a breadth of experience that they need to become rounded human beings having a range of ways of looking at the world, behaving amongst strangers and friends and integrating with others.

Some of the children at Red Balloon have only one 'outfit'. That 'outfit' is supposed to fit all situations. However, if we take that analogy of clothes as mirroring how people behave we soon realize that one set of clothes like one set of behaviours is very limiting. As an educator, I want all children to have a full suitcase with a range of different outfits to wear. From the casual to the smart and from the sporty to the professional. Similarly I want the children to have a suitcase with a range of ways of behaving to suit different situations; from assertive to conciliatory; from interested to politely unconcerned; from caring to being able to use 'tough love'; from friendly to polite and respectful. Of course the trick is not just having the suitcase but being able to use the right outfits for the appropriate occasions.

In classrooms and in the home reflecting on not only the child's behaviour, but on our own, helps children compile their own dictionary of behaviour as they would a wardrobe of clothes.

Stereotyping

Not being able to deal with bullying – especially when it is directed at one's sexuality – is one of the things the children we have had over the years at Red Balloon have in common.

Children who have been picked on for not conforming to their sexual stereotype find it hard to fight back. Being a girl and being called a boy, or being a boy and being called a girl hits hard at a child's identity.

We are a society that likes to know if a child is male or female or indeed if an adult is a man or a woman. Often the first question relatives ask of the new baby is – is it a girl or a boy? We like to know, we like to put the new baby into a category; do we buy it a blue bunny or a pink one! Children whose sexual stereotyping is not as marked as others can come in for relentless bullying.

Tomboys are one such category but on the whole our society is pretty tolerant of girls who like to wear trousers, climb trees and play football. We are far less tolerant of boys who enjoy playing with dolls, wearing dresses and using make-up, as in Cameron's story (see p.126).

To be constantly bullied over years for one reason begins to pall after a while. For some children who bully, the excitement is in the fireworks that erupt from the target, providing a spectacle for everyone.

Anger management

This manifestation of anger is a trademark of many bullied children. They are angry at the injustice of the situation, the apathy of the teachers to do anything serious about it, the impotence of adults to tackle the behaviour appropriately and to protect them from this onslaught, the dishonesty of the head-teacher who says 'all bullying is dealt with in this school' when the child knows theirs was not. Anger is one of the many forms of release that these bullied children have.

WHAT WE DO AT RED BALLOON

At Red Balloon anger management is one of the areas that is dealt with through the Personal and Social Education Programme.

Discussing how each one of us deals with anger is often brought to Circle Time. The children need to realize that all of us, including teachers, can get angry and that we have to find ways of dealing with this anger appropriately. Lists are made of what makes different people angry. Then there are discussions about recognizing the signs when you are about to boil over, recognizing the triggers that tap into your anger so that you can find a way to remove yourself from the situation. There are also discussions on what behaviours are always inappropriate, however angry you feel about taunting, mimicking, verbal abuse, sarcasm, name-calling or putdowns. Hitting people, throwing objects at people, grabbing people round the neck or punching them in the face are all unacceptable and if done as an adult could constitute a criminal offence. This is made very clear at Red Balloon.

During some of the personal and social sessions, discussions about how to dissolve anger are held and teachers and staff readily share with the children how they deal with their anger. Some describe how listening to music or going for a run, or taking the dog for a walk, or phoning a friend, or going to the cinema are real ways in which one's emotional outbursts can be channelled into appropriate activities whether you are a child or an adult.

WHAT TEACHERS AND PARENTS/CARERS CAN DO

For many adults, let alone children, issues of anger are never truly met head on. Warnings of, 'Daddy is angry, stay away from him' or 'Mum is in a bit of a temper, leave her alone', are examples of where parents duck the issue of anger rather than helping children understand this emotion.

Whilst these may be factual statements containing useful advice of staying away and leaving people alone it does not address the issue of 'When I am angry how should I deal with my anger?'

Acknowledging that all people get angry, with other people, with situations, with themselves, and finding appropriate ways of dealing with these feelings is something that young people need to learn about. Who better than their parents to help them understand these issues?

Separating behaviour out from a person is something that is important too. 'You are a naughty girl' is not very helpful and does not help a child understand why they have been 'naughty'. 'When you deliberately stamped on the plants I had just planted, that was very naughty behaviour, and I do not want you to do that again' at least tells the child the behaviour that was considered 'naughty'.

'Naughty' behaviour can be addressed and changed. Being naughty cannot. So as a parent when dealing with anger that results in aggressive, disruptive or destructive behaviour there are two strands that need dealing with separately. One is the emotions; the other is the behaviour.

Whether in the home or at school when dealing with the emotions the parent or teacher needs to focus on the feelings associated with being angry. So useful questions are: When you get angry what do you feel? How does it make you want to behave? What do you feel like doing? Encouraging the child to articulate their feelings helps them to understand them. Share how you feel too when you are angry. Explain how your body reacts: I get red in the face, my palms feel sweaty, I get a funny feeling in my tummy. All these physical reactions to getting angry help children realize that we all feel like that sometimes.

When dealing with the behaviour it needs to be made clear that children have choices. They chose to stamp on the plants or they chose not to. They chose to kick and bite or they removed themselves from that situation and chose to walk away. Asking them what 'good' choices they have made and listing them helps remind a child that there is not only one way of behaving when angry, frustrated or in a rage. What things can you do that are acceptable when you think you might be getting angry? may be another way to defuse the situation. What is unacceptable behaviour?

So in discussing anger management perhaps a parent and a teacher in a class can work out a range of 'safe' choices the child can make which will have the benefit of defusing the anger and not have the additional factor of being behaviour that leads to another sanction.

4

Mark's Story

Mark was 15 at the time of the interview.

'There wasn't a lot of physical stuff – they were clever like that – but if ever there was a bit of rough play going on, I'd get kicked really viciously or grabbed by the neck until I was gasping for breath.'

Even at primary school there were always gangs. There were the smart kids, the non-triers, the mess-about kids and the football fanatics. I was with the mess-about kids – we always played up in the classroom and we had a lot of fun out of school, too. Our group all grew up together, right from Reception.

When the time came to go to secondary school, only two of my good friends were going to the same school as me. It was one of the top local schools and we were lucky to get in. Unfortunately, I missed all the special days where the new kids got to know each other because I was away on holiday with my mum.

So when I started at the new school I didn't know anyone except my two mates from the old school. One of them was in the same class and he was really good to me. He looked out for me and made sure I knew what to do and where to go.

But not knowing the others from the start was a disadvantage. It's amazing how quickly the kids get together in groups, right from the moment they meet each other and they stick in a bunch and they can be suspicious and unfriendly towards a newcomer.

They turn away from you.

If you're not part of a gang, you're nothing. If you're not part of a gang there's no one to stick up for you and protect you. It's not good being on the outside.

Although we had our little groups at primary school, the gangs at secondary school were much stronger and more important. And even stronger than the ones inside the school were the ones on the outside – the local, territorial gangs. If you were a part of one of these, you were somebody. You had respect.

Most of all I wanted to be accepted by one of the local gangs – they were the ones to get into – but I knew it wouldn't be easy.

I had one advantage, though, over other hopefuls: I've always loved music – especially rap – and I was pretty good at it; I'd practise all the time and my rhythm and my patter got better and better. People listened and I began to be noticed.

Music is often a really important part of gang culture; it certainly is in North London where I come from.

Then I had a breakthrough. When I was in Year 8, someone mentioned me to his gang leader and I was asked to do some rap in front of the leader and the other gang members.

I was nervous because I really wanted them to like me and what I did, but I was confident, too. I knew I was good.

They all stood about, looking cool, but I could tell they were listening because some of them were tapping out the beat with their feet. When I'd finished, they were grinning and nodding their heads.

The leader came up to me: 'Yeah,' he said, and he punched me lightly on the arm. 'Yeah, you're good.' This was high praise, so I knew then that he was impressed.

'OK, you're in,' he said, and I'd never heard such sweet words. I was on cloud nine.

At last! I was accepted into the gang. And not just any gang, one of the outside strong local gangs. I was well pleased because in this gang you either had to be really good at music or be a really strong personality who people would follow and respect.

It's the same in lots of the other gangs in London.

I want to say something about gangs. People think they are all bad, but they're not. The great thing about being in a gang is the unity. You're all together, you belong, it makes you smile and feel good to be a part of it.

Of course, there's some hostility between gangs. Mostly they have beefs about stepping on each other's territory. Sometimes, this hostility can become the whole reason for the gang's existence and that's bad. Although I was a member of this one gang, my home was in the territory of a different gang so I had to keep my head down and go carefully. Round my home it didn't do to advertise the fact that I was with a gang from another territory.

This fighting over territory doesn't go back that far. It hasn't always been like this. A lot of the territorial stuff has come over from America where the bad things happened between the Crips and the Bloods. London gangs have copied them and some even call themselves Crips or Bloods.

Don't get me wrong, we weren't exactly angels in our gang. When I joined I was an innocent and I was uncomfortable about some of the bad stuff we did. Word would go round. 'We're going to nick stuff from that shop.'

We worked as a team. Someone distracting, someone looking out, others pocketing the stuff.

Then again: 'We're going to start a rumble at the cinema. No chickening out!'

Someone would begin the rumble and then we'd all join in.

I soon understood how things worked. If one person in the gang did anything then we all had to do it. We all stuck together and there was no chickening out.

But the buzz was fantastic. When we'd pulled something off – got away with it – we'd have a good laugh, punch the air and slap each other on the back. There was such a feeling of solidarity.

I never told my mum about the bad stuff; she was just pleased I had so many friends!

She was right. I had a load of friends. My blood brothers, my gang. All for one and one for all.

It was going well. I was in, I was respected and I was good friends with the top man – the gang leader.

One night my mum was going out so I invited the gang leader and another guy over to my house to stay the night. I was well pleased that they'd accepted and was looking forward to having them at mine.

But then things turned sour. The gang leader phoned all the other members and invited them to come, too.

Suddenly the whole gang were in my house, looking at my things, picking stuff up, laughing, pointing and lounging about on our furniture.

'Hey, great PlayStation,' said the gang leader.

Another guy picked up some photos of my family and starting laughing and showing them round to the others.

I snatched the photos back. 'Leave them alone!'

They were bouncing on the chairs and flinging stuff on the floor. I began to get mad. And I was scared, too. Were they going to trash my house? I could feel the tears coming and I wiped them away angrily, afraid someone might see them.

'You've got to get them out of here,' I yelled at the gang leader. 'I didn't ask them over.'

He looked at me with dead eyes. I could tell he was angry when I shouted at him in front of the others and when he replied he was icy calm. 'I thought you understood how we work,' he said smoothly, looking at his fingernails. 'We're a gang. We do things together.'

I looked round wildly, putting things back where they'd been disturbed. Pretty soon the others were taunting me, deliberately messing things up, dancing round me, holding up Mum's precious ornaments and stuff, pretending to drop them. My anger and shouting made things worse.

'Poor little boy. He's gonna cry!'

'Why're you so upset? Afraid your mum will be cross with you?'

'Mummy's boy!'

I had no control over them. They just laughed at me.

'Relax, man,' said one. But how could I relax when they were making such a mess in my house? My mum would kill me.

I began to feel really uncomfortable. It wasn't what I wanted. Having the gang leader and one other guy over was one thing. Having all the guys there causing havoc was a whole different ballgame. They could do some serious damage.

'Get out!' I yelled at them. I know my voice was hysterical. 'Get out of my house.'

But they took no notice.

'You've got to get them out of here,' I yelled at the gang leader.

I tried to phone my dad (he doesn't live with us) to get him to come over, but I couldn't get through to him.

And I kept on yelling at them to leave.

'You've gotta go! My mum's coming back. You gotta go!'

By this time I was really worked up and worried about what would happen.

'OK, OK, we'll go. It's no fun here anyway. You're so sad.'

Eventually they left – but I knew by then that I'd blown it with the gang.

I started to tidy up. How could they make such a mess in such a short time? There was stuff all over the floor, they'd taken food and drink from the fridge. Nothing was where it should be.

And then I noticed something else.

My PlayStation had gone!

I knew it was the gang leader who had taken it. I remembered the look on his face when he saw it: 'Great PlayStation.'

I was certain it was him. He'd taken it as an act of revenge! I'd made him look bad in front of the others by yelling at him and telling him to clear off – so he'd nicked my PlayStation.

This was his way of getting back at me.

If I was angry with him before, I was as mad as hell now.

I kicked at the wall, I thumped my fists on the table, and I yelled and swore.

'How *could* he take it?'

I ranted and raved and stomped around the house in a rage.

'The bastard! I'll get even with him,' I muttered, over and over.

And suddenly I thought of a way I *could* get even with him. If I hadn't been so angry and upset, if I'd been thinking clearly, I wouldn't have done it, but I was beyond reason. I just wanted to hit him where it hurt most.

I knew his girlfriend and I knew how to get in touch with her. I sat down at the computer.

'There's stuff you should know,' I said to her. 'This is what your boyfriend says about you. This is what he tells his gang about you.'

Then I listed all the rubbish things he'd said to us about her. About her family, about her figure, her face, her clothes, her temper. He often badmouthed her in front of us or told us about kinky stuff they did together. I don't know if any of it was true and I didn't care. I just wanted her to see him for what he was – a thief and a two-faced liar. I wanted her to drop him and spread rumours about him. I told her about him getting the whole gang over to my house and about stealing my PlayStation.

And before I had time to regret it, I hit the 'send' button.

I wanted revenge!

But about ten minutes after I sent the message to her, I realized how stupid I'd been.

It was a *big* mistake.

Of course, she got straight on to him and told him – word for word – everything I'd told her.

If I hadn't sent that message, perhaps things would have been OK. Perhaps I could have mended some fences, got back in with the gang.

But from the moment she let on what I'd said about the leader, I was marked.

I was a grass, a snake. Word went round all the local schools that I'd betrayed a gang member – the leader even.

Although I wasn't sure I really wanted to be in that gang any more, not being a part of it was much worse.

Now that I was labelled a grass, all the gang members tormented me.

They gave me death stares and they'd wait for me outside after school.

'Snitch.'

'Grass.'

'Snake.'

There wasn't a lot of physical stuff – they were clever like that – but if ever there was a bit of rough play going on, I'd get kicked really viciously or grabbed by the neck until I was gasping for breath.

There were threats, too.

'Snakes get stamped on.'

'We're watching you.'

It got so that I dreaded what might happen to me. I was made to feel really uncomfortable and wherever I went – in or out of school – there was always this scary uncertainty of what might happen to me the next day, the next hour, the next minute.

Walking down the road, I'd sense someone creeping up behind me and I'd whip round, ready for a rumble, my heart thumping with fear.

Sometimes they'd crowd in on me and jostle me, sometimes they'd just go on walking behind me laughing at me and shouting out names. Horrible, hurtful names.

I'd never been hated like this before. Nearly everyone turned away from me and although I still had some friends it was hard for them to support me because then they got grief, too.

It went on like this, day after day after day. In the end it really gets to you and you can't cope with it. I began to shrivel up, shutting down emotions that were too raw to deal with.

How can you be a happy confident person with a load of friends one day, swaggering about, doing stuff with your gang, getting a buzz from their company and then, suddenly, be so alone?

I used to come out of school surrounded by friends, now I came out on my own, avoided by almost everyone. Stared at, whispered at, laughed at.

What did I feel then? It's hard to describe.

You turn in on yourself when this happens. You become a sort of brain dead zombie. I couldn't concentrate. My days were full of dread, waiting for what might happen at break times or after school. And at night I'd have really scary dreams about what they'd do to me the next day. I was too full of fear to enjoy anything. I couldn't enjoy my food; I couldn't even enjoy my music.

But I thought they'd get bored with taunting me. I thought, if I kept my head down, it would get better.

Wrong!

It got a lot worse.

I suppose I should have realized that when I started to dress in white, this would make me an even better target for them. But I *had* to dress. It is all part of my religion – the year of initiation. And you have to keep your head covered with a white hat.

When I first put the clothes on I was proud of them but, as you can imagine, they really stood out at school.

But the moment I walked through the school gates and saw the other kids staring at me and whispering, my pride in my special clothes dissolved.

'Look at him! What is he now? Some sort of bloody angel?'

Being rubbished because I'd betrayed another gang member was bad enough, but being rubbished because of my religion was much worse.

Everything I'd been brought up to believe in was treated as some sort of joke. It was as if my whole family were being held up to ridicule.

The gang members poked fun at me (though I have to admit that there was one guy who stood up for me). And they taunted me most for wearing my hat.

They'd snatch it off my head and fling it on the ground and stamp on it and when I bent down to pick it up, they'd shove me so I stumbled and fell.

And when they walked past me they'd hit me on the head.

'Cool hat!' they'd say, sniggering.

It was this rubbishing of my religion that really got to me.

And one day, I just knew I couldn't take any more of it. My head was messed up and my body was reacting, too. I was tired all the time, my limbs were heavy and my brain wouldn't work. I'd never felt like this before and it made me really scared. Everything was going to pieces.

It was then that I told Mum what was happening. About being laughed at for my white clothes and about all the stuff that had gone before.

Mum was brilliant. She knew I'd been stressed but she never realized how bad it had got because I'd refused to talk about it. Now, at last, she understood what I'd been going through.

'You're not going back to that school,' she said firmly. 'I'm not having you tormented like this. You'll have lessons at home.'

It was such a relief when she said that. My whole body suddenly slumped with relief and I started crying. I couldn't stop myself. I sobbed and sobbed and when at last I got myself together again, I felt a whole heap better.

Mum was on my side and she understood. It was a good feeling.

I didn't mind being alone. It was great to be away from the constant taunting, the fear, and the dread of what might happen round the next corner, in the next break time.

For a while we tried home schooling but it didn't really work out. Mum and I were on top of each other too much and we kept rowing.

We'd reached a bad place. Home schooling wasn't working and there was no way I was going back to my old school or any of the other local schools – whichever school I went to they'd know about me.

Then my Gran heard about Red Balloon and that a Centre was opening in North London.

When Mum first told me about Red Balloon I said that there was no way I would go to *any* other school *ever*. But she kept going on about it and eventually she persuaded me to go along to an interview, just to see what it was like. Once I started talking to the staff here, I realized how different it was.

It's just an ordinary house – not like a school at all. More like a club. It's a safe place to be and no one taunts you.

I'm kept busy and, best of all, there's nothing to get in a feud about with the other students. I'll stay here until I leave school.

I get on well with most of the staff and I look on them as friends more than teachers. I'm better at trusting the right people now.

I still see my old gang members sometimes but I don't get grief from them any more. Although I acknowledge them when we pass in the street I don't stop and talk.

I haven't turned my back on gangs, though. I'm still really interested in them and I understand how they work. I know about all the London gangs – by word of mouth and by going online.

Gangs can be good. I met this guy at a singing group who's from South London. He's a really great guy and I trust him like I've never trusted anyone before. He hangs around with the South London Latino gangs. They don't do stupid things and they are much more like a family. Once you're their family, you're always their family.

I want to study music at GCSE and I want to make a career in music if I can. Also, when I leave school I really want to travel round the Spanish speaking countries – Spain, South America, Cuba. I speak a bit of Spanish and I want to learn more.

COMMENTS FROM RED BALLOON STAFF

Things have changed considerably since the time of this interview. The pull of a new gang proved too strong and Mark left Red Balloon. He dealt with his decision to leave maturely, came in and spoke to the staff calmly and then came back another day and said goodbye to everyone. This way the door has been left open for him to have Red Balloon's support should he need it in the future.

DISCUSSION

Carrie Herbert and Tracey Doran

Gangs

Gangs, gang culture and the modus operandi of gangs in the twenty-first century, it could be argued, is an organized form of bullying. The coercion and fear that is associated with how the various members of a gang interact is based on a rigid hierarchy of intimidation, threats and conformity. This powerful form of socialization constitutes bullying.

Gangs of youths have increased their use of violence in the last 50 years in Britain. Originally formed as a means of self-protection for families and friends within a neighbourhood, many gangs had good intentions, but today's gangs are often nothing more than groups of bullies preying on vulnerable isolated victims or intimidating a community. As they expand and proliferate they mimic their American heroes and increasingly use guns and knives to threaten their victims and to protect themselves.

Often children will join a gang because they have an overwhelming desire to 'belong', to be part of and to have a place within a group. Their families, the school environment, the church, and other youth clubs are seemingly no longer fulfilling that role.

Unfortunately, though, as well as the need to 'belong', many children join gangs as a way of protecting themselves from bullying and violence. It is their hope that if they are members of one gang then bullies from another gang will probably understand the reciprocation that will occur if they attack them and that they will be 'safe' and 'protected'.

In 2003 the Youth Justice Board conducted a survey of 5000 young people aged 11–16 about crime and school. Half of these interviewed stated that they had been a victim of crime and 60 per cent expressed serious concern about the level of violence at school and in their community. The head of the Youth Justice Board, Lord Warner, when talking about young people who join gangs said 'It's a case of "if you can't beat them, join them".' Far from a gang being a form of liberation, this level of fear has the effect of drawing young people into a gang's clutches, making them a prisoner in a territory that has to be defended and identifying them as a target by their association.

The ideology of belonging to a gang, and the myth that is peddled to young people that being a loyal member brings with it the promise of protection, support and help is patently untrue. The reality of gang membership is that it perpetuates the violence, the warfare and the territory defending to the detriment of the welfare of a young person and in some cases may cause their death.

There is an example of this in the shooting of Rhys Jones. Rhys was an innocent young boy of 11 who got caught in the crossfire between two gang members. One of the members of the Croxteth Crew gang (the gang who killed Rhys) was forced to play a part in the cover up of the crime.

Boy X was 16 at the time of the shooting and was a vulnerable young man who had joined the gang for protection. He was only a peripheral member but on the evening of the accidental murder, Rhys's killer went to Boy X's house after the shooting and forced him to hide the murder weapon. Boy X was too scared to refuse even though he soon realized what he was hiding. In case he should go to the police, the gang made veiled threats to both him and his family and kept up constant low-level intimidation. However, after five months, Boy X did go to the police and in return for his testimony, since his evidence was so valuable, he was offered immunity from prosecution, an identity change and a move away from Croxteth.

This sort of pressure is just one example of a young person joining a gang for protection only to be bullied to the point of criminal activity and family intimidation.

WHAT TEACHERS AND PARENTS/CARERS CAN DO

The simple answer is that there is no failsafe method for stopping a young person joining a gang but here are a few guidelines:

- Belonging is important to us all. Spending time with each of your children every day, showing them affection, making them feel special and making sure they understand how significant they are to the family is a central part of ensuring a sense of belonging.
- Children are attracted to gangs by their offer of friendship and support. Start teaching your children early, from the age of four or five, that gangs are dangerous and do not provide positive support or role models.
- Teach your children what to do if a gang member approaches them. The best response is to walk away and tell an adult.
- Know your children's friends and families. Invite your children's friends home to share your family life and to be part of a wider family community. Keep track of your children's whereabouts at all times and set definite boundaries and curfews for your children's outside activities.
- Children with a history of academic failure are at high risk. If your child has learning difficulties, work together with his or her teachers. Seek help from tutors and help your child with his or her homework.

- Schools can help by offering programmes about gang culture as part of their PSHE (Physical, Social and Health Education) lessons. Make sure that you speak to the school as soon as you have any concerns. Also notify the head-teacher if you are concerned that children from your son's or daughter's school are talking about gangs. Adults can address the issues of gangs if they are aware of their presence.

Though the steps above offer no magic solution, they may make gangs appear less attractive and prepare young people to more effectively resist gang pressure to join.

Bullying because of religious belief

Religion is another sort of belonging – belonging to a group who believe in a particular god, set of rituals, clothes, mantra or set of rules. Young people who are brought up to believe something that is different from their peers are often ridiculed and humiliated for those beliefs in a place where diversity and difference is not celebrated. At Red Balloon we try to allow each child to express their beliefs and values and have them respected by other Red Balloon children. Take for example this conversation that happened in the Community Room one day. Overheard by the Housekeeper it went something like this:

John: Ryan, do you believe in God?

Ryan: Yes.

John: Why? I don't.

Ryan: Because my mum and dad do and that is what I have been taught.

John: What is God to you?

Ryan: He's someone looking out for you all the time.

John: How do you know He is there?

Ryan: You don't, but I sometimes pray for Him to help me. For example if I have a problem that I don't know the answer to I just pray that God will help me sort it out.

John: How do you know it works?

Ryan: Well about 20 minutes after the prayer I get the answer. It just pops into my head and I know that God has helped me.

This conversation took place in front of a number of children. All respected Ryan's ideas even though they were very different from their own. Teaching children to respect and not ridicule is an important part of growing up.

WHAT TEACHERS AND PARENTS/CARERS CAN DO

Britain is a multi-cultural society in which there are a range of religious beliefs, practices and traditions. Being tolerant of different races and religions is as much a part of the tolerant home environment as it is of the classroom.

There are many opportunities in lessons, other than Religious Studies, such as English, History, Citizenship and Personal and Social Education for teachers to make sure race and religion are highlighted in discussions, studies and class projects. Novels that discuss alternative lifestyles, that are set in other countries or that tell stories about different nationalities working together provide a way to understand more about different races, local traditions and cultures, helping to make young people more rounded, more accepting and more tolerant.

Prevention is obviously better than cure. So creating a classroom (and home) where racism or pejorative comments about religion are acceptable creates an environment that is unsafe for learning and living. It is clear that children are not born racist. It is also true that they are not born belonging to any particular religion. So religious beliefs and racist practices are both examples of learned behaviour. Children will learn to be racist if they live in a racist family or are a member of a class where racist views are tolerated. The same with religion. If a child is a member of a family that belongs to a particular religious group they will learn those beliefs, traditions and cultures. This should not be to the exclusion of others' religions and, as with attitudes to sexuality, each child is encouraged to be inclusive not exclusive.

5

Lauren's Story

Lauren was 16 at the time of the interview.

> 'I walked in at 9 o'clock on that first day, that September morning, all ready and raring to go. By 3 o'clock I just wanted to go home, tuck up into bed and cry. The older children had ripped my uniform and me to shreds.'

When I was six years old, my best friend Sarah was murdered. Well, maybe murdered is a bit strong. She was so badly treated – and neglected – by her step mum that she got really ill and died. It was a terrible case and there was lots about it in the papers.

Sarah's death shattered me. We'd always done things together, ever since we were very little. She was my best friend in the whole world.

I suppose, looking back, it was then that I began to feel isolated from other children at school. I was so raw and I was very wary about making friends again. But although I didn't really get on with my contemporaries at primary school and I was a bit lonely, no one picked on me there and I did well at my lessons.

Things changed, though, as soon as I got to secondary school. I was nervous but excited. I loved to learn and couldn't wait for all the new educational challenges ahead. I pulled my long white socks up, tied my hair in my pink band and pulled my skirt down to my knees. I was a normal school girl in regulation school uniform. Right…? Wrong.

I walked in at 9 o'clock on that first day, that September morning, all ready and raring to go. By 3 o'clock I just wanted to go home, tuck up into bed and cry. The older children had ripped my uniform and me to shreds.

'Pull your skirt up!'

I walked in at 9 o'clock on that first day, that
September morning, all ready and raring to go.

'Pull your socks down!'

'You're frigid!'

I really don't know why these older kids picked on me particularly, but once they'd identified me as a target, they never stopped taunting me. I wanted to fit in – and I tried to – but by that time it was too late.

I suppose I was a bit innocent and shy. I was really intimidated by this older gang.

Going home on the school bus, right from the very first day, they started laughing at me and calling out:

'You look horrible.'

'You look like my nan!'

'You're a skank.'

So I tried to conform. I changed my uniform. I experimented with make-up and short skirts and hair dos, but this only gained me new names like slag and whore. It hurt. The names weren't too bad at first but when it happens all day, every day it just wears you down, chipping away at who you are. Then the physical stuff began, being spat at, slapped or pushed – and worse.

There was this one boy who would come and sit next to me on the school bus and start touching me. And everyone else would urge him on, laughing when I tried to make him stop.

Going to and from school became hell. Sometimes I was too frightened to go on the bus so Mum would drive me to school. But she couldn't do it every day.

I had chewing gum put in my hair and one girl even pushed me right in front of the bus as it was moving off.

Break and lunchtimes were terrible too. The boy who tormented me on the bus spat in my food so I couldn't eat it. And once he and some mates found a condom and threw it at me.

Mum and Dad went to see the deputy head of Year 7 after the spitting business and made a complaint. The boy admitted spitting in my food but he was just given a break time detention; but he did more or less leave me alone after that.

About halfway through Year 7 I was allowed to change school buses and at least the journey to and from school was better.

The other incidents went on building up, though. By now, my year group had turned against me, copying the older children. Group activities were miserable. No one would include me and I was left out of everything until the teacher insisted they let me join in. And that made it even worse.

I found the work easy, but this isolated me even more. 'Nerd!' was whispered round the classroom whenever a teacher praised me.

I felt so alone and soon lost interested in my schoolwork. What good was it being clever if you felt as though you were going to end up dead? I never thought I would even see my sixteenth birthday things got so bad. No one truly understands how it feels to be tortured everyday you walk through those school gates, like a baby lamb going to the slaughter-house, your heart thumping against your chest, your palms sweaty and your head numb with fear.

Mum and Dad were always going into the school and the deputy head promised that the head-teacher would be informed and that the bullying would be dealt with. We found out, much later, that the head was never told anything about my situation. The deputy head of Year 7 didn't take my problems seriously and said I was just a drama queen.

I struggled on, then halfway through Year 8, a group of girls cornered me outside the sports centre. They had a knife and they were threatening to use it on me. I was terrified. I knew they meant it.

I shall never forget the sight of that knife, its blade glinting in the sunlight as it came closer and closer. I twisted away from it but they held me down, laughing at me, taunting me.

'Scared, are you?'

The knife came closer and I tried to scream but someone held a hand over my mouth.

'Not so clever now, are you?'

'We're going to kill you. We hate you!'

Whimpering, I managed to twist round and struggle free. I ran for my life.

I reported them. And that made my life even worse.

'Why did you tell?' they yelled at me. 'We didn't even touch you. Grow up!'

Life got a bit better when I joined the army cadets. There were older people there and I made a group of friends. Some of them went to my school and it was the first time I started to feel a part of something. There was a boy at army cadets. He was 18 and he was kind to me. He protected me and I felt he really liked me.

But one day, this boy invited me over to his mate's house. Right from the moment I walked through the door, I sensed something wasn't right. His friend was much older – in his thirties – and there was something pervy about him. But they were both really nice to me and complimented me and said how pretty I was. Then the friend gave me some alcohol and I drank it. I wanted to seem cool and grown up but I wasn't used to it and I started to feel ill. And then suddenly, everything changed. My head was swimming and my legs were wobbly and the men were on top of me.

They did horrible things to me.

When at last I got home, I couldn't tell my mum what had happened. I felt dirty and ashamed.

I was very on edge at school – all over the place – and in the end I went to see the school nurse and told her what had happened.

After this the police were called in and social services. Although I said nothing to anyone else at school, I was constantly missing lessons and presenting these yellow slips to my teachers that said I was to be excused.

For some reason, in that school the yellow slips have always been associated with pregnancy.

Rumours went flying round and the taunting became unbearable.

'Slut!'

It was my fault that I was taller, had curly hair
and was the target for bullies.

'Skank.'

At about this time I started to cut myself. It was the only way I could get any relief from the tension and muddle in my head.
I hated going through the police interviews. I hated having to tell them what happened.

In the end, both men were arrested and sentenced.

I didn't go back to school after that. I couldn't face it. I left in May and spent a lonely time at home.

At the beginning of the next school year I went to another secondary school. It was quite a long way from my home and I thought it would be a new start.

I couldn't have been more wrong. The problems followed me; the children from my old school just rang their friends and told them to look out for me. None of the teachers understood and none of them wanted to help. They accused *me* of being the problem! It was my fault that I was taller, had curly hair and was the target for the bullies. I was in the wrong for being a victim!

Soon the taunts began again:

'Slut!'

'Skank!'

'Look at her frizzy hair.'

'Her boobs are bigger than mine!'

Despite this, I made some good friends, but I had trouble with some of the kids who were into drugs and I was always scared they might beat me up.

I met a nice boy at the new school. He had trouble with the druggie kids, too. We started going out together and I felt happy with him.

One day, I went to my friend Zoe's place after school. In the evening we went out. We weren't doing anything, just walking along a road. There's nothing much to do there anyway, it's right out in the country, in the middle of nowhere.

It was very quiet; there was nothing on the road and we were just chatting about this and that. Then gradually I became aware of a noise puncturing the country sounds of the wind and the birds. It was very faint at first but all the time it got louder and louder as it came nearer; a deep throaty sound. I looked behind me and saw a motorbike coming up the road, revving and roaring like a hungry monster. I don't know why, but as soon as I saw the motorbike, I had a really bad feeling in my gut and my heart started racing.

The roaring came nearer and nearer and suddenly the motorbike was beside us, skidding to a halt in front of us, barring our way, still throbbing noisily.

There was this boy riding it and as I looked up, scared, I met his eyes. I didn't know him at all. He was a lot older than us. I hated the way he looked at me.

'Get on,' he said, pointing at the pillion seat.

I shrank back behind Zoe. He kept on staring at me.

'C'mon, prostitute. Get up behind me.'

Prostitute! My whole body shrank with fear at the word.

Zoe found her voice. 'Go away!' she shouted.

'Go away, leave us alone,' I added, but my voice came out as a pathetic whisper.

Then he pulled a knife out from the back pocket of his jeans.

He kept staring at me as he showed us the knife.

'If you don't get on this bike,' he said to me, 'I'm going to stab your friend.'

He reached over and grabbed my arm. 'Get on!' he hissed.

By this time, Zoe was sobbing, stumbling away down the road.

I tried to twist away from him but he was too strong for me. He had my arm in a vice-like grip and, all the time, I could see the knife in his other hand. I was too scared to resist as he shoved me up onto the back of the bike, opened the throttle and roared off.

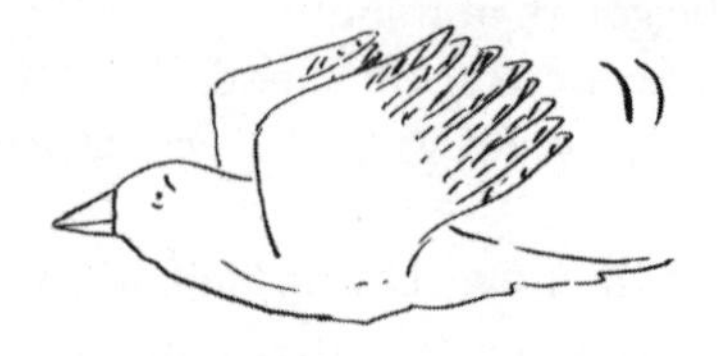

A blackbird flew out of the hedge in front of us…I watched it fly up into the sky and envied its freedom.

I shall never, ever, forget that journey.

My whole body was shaking and my legs felt like jelly. I'd never been on a motorbike before; I was scared I'd fall off and I was even more scared about what the boy was going to do to me.

I watched the trees and hedges flash past as he drove on, faster and faster. If only someone would come up the road! But there was no one. The road remained bleak and empty. I wanted to throw myself off the bike but if I did, I knew he'd just come back for me; there was no one to rescue me from him. A blackbird flew out of the hedge in front of us, squawking with fear, and I watched it fly up into the sky and envied its freedom.

He drove on and on until we reached a barn which was miles from anywhere then he parked the bike and dragged me off the pillion.

'Come on, tart!'

Tart! Is that what they all think of me?

I was shaking so much that I could hardly stand and he had to drag me towards the barn.

And that's where he raped me. Behind the barn.

When he'd finished, he let me go.

'If you tell anyone, I'll come after you and stab you,' he said.

Then he drove off.

I was shaking and crying. My clothes were stained and I felt really sore. I stumbled to the road and started to make my way back.

It wasn't long before Zoe's parents found me. She had phoned them and asked them to come and pick us up. Zoe was still crying. She felt so guilty that she'd left me.

'I'm so sorry,' she said, again and again.

But I was completely traumatized. I couldn't reply.

This time I told my mum right away what had happened and Zoe and I made a statement to the police.

My parents had a meeting with the school. They knew that my attacker's brother was at the school and they wanted the school to promise I'd be safe.

Of course, the story got out somehow although I certainly didn't say anything. Girls started to take the boy's side.

'I know him. He'd never do that. You're lying.'

'You're a slut anyway. You asked for it, prostitute.'

I was spat at, kicked, my hair pulled.

And every time I reported this, the teachers didn't believe me. No one seemed to believe me.

Once, a girl slapped me across the face right in front of a security camera. I told my form teacher but she didn't believe me until I insisted they look at the film in the camera. They had to believe me then.

If possible, the bullying was worse than at my first school. I had tons of time off, alone and miserable at home.

But I wanted to learn. I didn't like missing lessons, so sometimes I'd force myself to go in.

Once a gang of kids chased me away. They chased me right out of the school gates and into the road.

'We don't want you here. You're a piece of shit. Go away. Go and kill yourself. We hate you. Everyone hates you.'

I ran out into the road. I saw the car coming towards me but I didn't stop. I wanted it all to end so I kept going.

Fortunately for me, the driver swerved and hit the brakes and just managed to avoid me. I'd missed being killed by a matter of inches.

A teacher was watching all of this. She said I wasn't chased. She said she'd told me to stop but I went on running.

The case against the boy who attacked me dragged on and on. I couldn't sleep for thinking about it. He said I'd wanted sex and that he hadn't raped me.

I stopped going to school. I was so down that I didn't think I had the strength to give evidence in court again. In the end, the case was dropped.

I was self-harming a lot by then and crying all the time. And drinking when I felt down. I was in such a mess. I hated myself and I thought I was worthless. I had some help from the people at ChildLine and Kidscape, but I still wanted to learn. I wanted to continue my education but I didn't know how I could. I'd already missed so much. I had no idea what was going to happen next. My school sent me a letter predicting my GCSE grades as Cs and Ds! That wasn't me! I was an A grade student, but with the bullying and uncaring teachers my education had suffered a terrible turn for the worse and was ruining my future. It had damaged the chances I had of getting into college and university, as well as any chance of having a normal life. Along with my physical scars there were emotional ones too in the form of post-traumatic stress disorder.

My parents spent hours on the computer trying to find help. Anything would do. I was offered a place at a pupil referral unit but that was not where I should be. That's where bullies are sent when they are kicked out of school.

I was emailed through some work but I didn't find sums like 3 + 5 challenging, surprisingly enough! Then my father had a breakthrough. A place called the Red Balloon Learner Centre popped up on the computer screen. It advertised itself as a school that helped recover bullied children. That's me I thought, that's exactly what I need.

Within a few weeks I had my first look around. It looked just like a normal house, very relaxed, cosy and safe. Everyone seemed really nice and helpful. This was the place for me. We had to fight with the county to get funding but after all that had happened to me they finally agreed and I started just before the summer holidays.

At first I was very unsure of myself and I was always waiting for someone to taunt me, tell me I was rubbish, laugh at me, but the teachers were lovely and gradually I became more confident and felt able to concentrate on my work again. And make friends.

My education got back underway and I started building positive trusting relationships with teachers and students for the first time ever. I actually enjoyed getting out of bed to go there. Red Balloon helped me to get my confidence and voice back. Thanks to them I entered public speaking competitions and have been to conferences with Carrie to speak about Red Balloon, something I just wouldn't have done before.

Red Balloon organizes activities during the summer for current and past students and at one of these I met Robert. He'd left Red Balloon but we found out we lived near each other and we started seeing each other. He was 18.

We went out from June until the following March and then we broke up. But by that time I was pregnant.

Having Abi has changed everything. She means the world to me and I adore her. I'm determined to protect her.

I took three GCSEs early as I soon caught up with my work and gained two As and a B before I was even Year 11. I added to that by gaining an A, two Bs and a C the following year.

The staff at Red Balloon never doubted that I was capable of anything less then As and Bs. They helped me through my PTSD and gave me confidence and a reason to live.

Care to Learn provides nursery care while you study, and my mum and dad have been great. Abi and I live with them now.

Quite simply, Red Balloon rescued me. Being able to study in safety and make new friends turned my life around. I know there may be problems in the future but at last I feel better about myself and more able to face them.

I now go to an independent sixth form college. Red Balloon received a scholarship from them and felt I deserved it. I'm well on my way to success and feel so grateful that I found Red Balloon when I did.

Just a reflection: I get the train into school every day and see the people who bullied me on the opposite platform. Funny really, they're all going to some hair and beauty course or to retake their GCSEs while I'm off to highflying Cambridge. The two tracks go in different directions, one leading to a dead end place and the other to an up and coming successful pathway that leads to anywhere I want to go – London, Oxford, the world. I know what platform I'm on and I'm so happy to be there. Red Balloon has helped me see that bullying hasn't ruined my life; it has affected my past but I'm not going to let it affect my future.

But without Red Balloon I could have died.

LAUREN'S DAD

While she was at primary school, Lauren was chatty and positive at home but from the very first day at secondary her personality started to change and she became withdrawn and depressed. She blamed us for sending her to school dressed wrongly but to us she just looked like a normal schoolgirl and, at the time, she was proud of her uniform. Lauren developed physically very early and I'm sure this made her vulnerable. Perhaps we should have taken more action than we did but we used to ring the school frequently and we went in to see her form teacher, too. But we got the impression that the school thought we were making a fuss about nothing. After the first sexual assault and the court case, we took Lauren away but the bullying continued at her new school.

By this time, Lauren was very depressed and had no self-esteem. She hated her family and she hated herself. She would write stuff on her bedroom wall.

'I'm rubbish.'

> 'I'm just a sex slave.'
>
> 'I want to die.'

We dreaded getting up in the morning in case she had killed herself during the night.

All this put a huge strain on family relationships but the birth of Abi has made a big difference and Lauren is a great mum. With the enormous and non-judgemental support she has received from Red Balloon and with having to be responsible for Abi, she is beginning to stabilize and look to the future. If it hadn't been for Red Balloon, though, I honestly don't think Lauren would still be alive.

She's turning out to be a bit of an entrepreneur and is making some money by buying and selling children's clothes and toys online. She's a bright girl and articulate. She made it to the regional finals of a public speaking competition which was a great boost to her morale.

COMMENTS FROM STAFF AT RED BALLOON

Having the baby has made a big difference to Lauren. She now has to take responsibility for someone else – someone to whom she needs to learn to give unconditional love and who will give her unconditional love.

Lauren's intellectual curiosity and her appetite for learning were very apparent. She has an excellent mind, the ability to engage with a subject, to self-edit and to see behind problems. She also has quite a flair for business.

Because she felt safe, Lauren thrived academically while she was with us, as the extracts from some of her achievement records below show:

> 'You have been juggling many challenges these past months, and you have coped with them successfully, at home, at school, and in your own dreams and aspirations. You are clever, resourceful and bold, and you have many talents. When you are relaxed and engaged, you can go to the heart of a problem with great liveliness, power and directness.'

> 'You have not only managed to work well, with passion, commitment and interest all this year, but you have also managed to do this bouncing back quickly from many successive crises, which will have cost you a lot in terms of emotional upheaval. You are so strong, and fragile at the same time.'

Other observations that crop up are:

> 'excellent analytical skills'
>
> 'intellectual hunger'
>
> 'ideas…sharp and stunning'
>
> 'subtle insights'
>
> 'vigorous explanations'.

Lauren became a valued member of the Red Balloon community. She joined in fully in corporate activities, made friends and was able to converse easily and politely with all groups. She participated in discussion and debate within the school and accepted others' points of view. As her fears subsided, she was able to empathize with the situations of other students and to support them.

Lauren is now at sixth form college working towards her A levels. It was not an easy transition, leaving Red Balloon and meeting a new set of students with the added strain of being a young mother. She frequently comes back to see the staff at Red Balloon.

DISCUSSION

Carrie Herbert

Sexual assault

Sexual assault is a particular kind of attack that not only saps one's self-worth but also has the ability to force a girl to grow up more quickly than she would otherwise.

Being more aware, having different attitudes, knowing more and having had adult experiences can set you apart from your peers. This in turn can lead someone to be singled out for special and adverse attention – or bullying.

Some young women who have been sexually attacked begin to see themselves as having value only in the sexual sphere. They flirt, giggle, behave inappropriately, have few personal boundaries and know how to excite men because that is what they know and that is the behaviour for which they have been rewarded in the past.

Not only are they targets for men, but also their peers begin to condemn, discuss and judge their behaviour. They are called sexual names (of which there are far more for women than there are for men), they are accused of being traitors to their sex, of letting down girls' and women's reputations and of being cheap. Yet these young people are stranded in a no-man's land, being on the one hand found alluring by some boys and men and on the other despised and ostracized by girls and women.

This will in turn have an effect on their relationships, their ability to have and maintain friendships, their confidence in their academic achievements, their ability to trust people, and all these may have an effect on their mental health.

WHAT WE DO AT RED BALLOON

At Red Balloon we do a lot of talking. There are therapists and counsellors around all the time and the children have an hour booked each week in which to work with such a professional on their own issues. Each teacher too has some level of skill in counselling. This is important if at the start of a lesson or even mid way through a lesson the student is unable to continue with their studies because they are overwhelmed with depression and lack of self-worth. The teacher may feel it is right to abandon the lesson and discuss what the problem is – or they may insist that the student do 'a bit more' then they can discuss the problem in detail. Talking is an essential part of a child's recovery. Reflecting on what happened, discussing different ways of talking about it, ways of dealing with it, the way other people dealt with a similar issue can all help a child move on.

One of the common features of children who have been bullied is aggression – to 'jump in and attack' before anyone else can. Getting the opponent on the defensive is a way of having the upper hand. Of course this comes from not trusting people and having to guard against a putdown, a criticism or a taunt.

Sexual bullying

Sexual bullying or harassment is one of the most under-reported yet common forms of bullying, mainly perpetrated by boys and aided and abetted by girls and usually directed towards one girl.

This case is a classic example. A student who is innocent, pretty, interested in her work and committed to learning and making progress is bullied by her peers. A nasty sexual assault happens and instead of being supported, cared for or protected by her own sex she is vilified, called a slut, accused of having provoked it, as they seek to drive her out of their community.

Sexual harassment is the kind of behaviour that is often overlooked in schools, starting at primary schools where boys chase girls around the playground, lift their skirts, try to kiss them and call them names while adults look on and say 'boys will be boys'. It is in this way that girls learn that they are expected to put up with this treatment, that if they complain they are called frigid, lezzies or whores.

In secondary schools I have witnessed humiliating behaviour in classrooms where teachers have asked a boy to 'give her one' – meaning a book – but the double entendre was explicit.

Another case which was covered up, not dealt with and resulted in the girl's attempted suicide was that of a Bulgarian student whose English was not fluent in coarse words. Asked by a boy if he could f..k her she said 'yes'. When he took her behind the school pavilion and told her to lie down she became suspicious and ran off. The boy put it around the school that she had had sex with him, she was a slag and an easy lay. No one would believe her story.

WHAT WE DO AT RED BALLOON

At Red Balloon the issue of sexual putdowns is taken very seriously. One way of making sure that girls and boys can have time to think about things that concern them is to have a girls' group and a boys' group. Taken by members of staff at different times it gives each group the opportunity to explore areas of sex and sexuality that they may find inhibiting in a mixed sex group. I was involved in many single sex discussions. The girls often wanted to talk about domestic violence, what it was, how it happened and what you could do about it if you found you were involved with a man who hit you, abused you, humiliated or sexually demeaned you.

In some of the programmes with the girls a more explicit feminist approach was taken where women's and girls' position in society was examined in more detail. Discussions about housework, equal pay, the glass ceiling and child-rearing were all put on the table as were the rights of women, emancipation and the suffrage movement.

For the boys, two of the recurring conversations were about 1) whether it was ever OK to hit your girlfriend and 2) what constituted consensual and non-consensual sex, i.e. rape.

In this way I think education can have a crucial influence on the role that young men and women play in society. As with drugs, alcohol and sex education so relationships, equality and sexual abuse are issues which need to be aired and where guidance should be given.

WHAT TEACHERS AND PARENTS/CARERS CAN DO

All of us know that racial harassment or bullying disabled people is wrong, cruel and indefensible – there is no contradiction here!

However, sexual activity covers conduct that being demonstrated by person A towards person B may be actively wanted, liked, sought and reciprocated by B. However, change A to C and the same behaviour is regarded by B as distasteful, unwanted, frightening and abusive. What has changed? The person!

I have witnessed at primary schools boys chasing girls with a ruler to look up their skirts. I have heard of boys being chased by older girls to be kissed. Is this child's play or is this unwanted sexual behaviour? Who decides?

Whatever the level of schooling it is important that children are taught that they have the right to decide for themselves that behaviour is wanted or unwanted. That a cuddle from Uncle John is not wanted but a cuddle from Mr Smith from next door is. That a child does not want to kiss Great Aunt Mabel but she does want to kiss Sally's mum. If we can allow children to use their sixth sense, their 'gut feeling' to make decisions about touching, patting, kissing and other intimate behaviours we will be providing them with a skill that they will use all their lives.

6

Zac's Story

Zac was 17 at the time of the interview.

> 'Every morning, before the teacher arrived, I knew what would happen. They'd be waiting for me... They'd pick up their weapons then. Anything that came to hand – long rulers, chairs, whatever – and hit me with them.'

I don't think anyone got at me when I was at primary school. As far as I remember I was pretty happy then.

It started when I went to middle school, the taunting and name-calling. Pretty well from day one. I've always been big and I guess I stood out among the smaller kids. And I was probably smarter than the rest of the class.

So that should have been a winning combination. I was big and I was smart.

Wrong! It was a bad combination.

Gradually, over the weeks and months that followed, I became the class victim, the one they all loved to hate.

To begin with I thought I could cope with all the constant verbals:

'Fatty.'

'Big boy.'

'Smart arse.'

I tried to shrug it off – to ignore it. But when it happened every single day I was at school it began to wear me down.

At first it was only a couple of boys but it soon became a class game and everyone was joining in.

And then it began to spread through the school. Some of the class above started calling me names – and even some of the younger kids thought it was clever to join in with what the older boys were doing. It's amazing how quickly a pack of kids pick up on this kind of thing, how rumours fly around and how soon most of the school seems to be turning against you.

The taunts followed me around wherever I went – at break time, between lessons, at lunchtime.

'Why haven't you got any friends, big boy?'

'No one likes you. Why don't you go and put your head in the toilet?'

Sometimes I answered back but that only seemed to make things worse so, in the end, I just kept quiet and retreated into my shell. I couldn't be bothered to retaliate; there wasn't any point.

They'd just laugh at me and repeat what I said or pull faces at me.

'OOOh! He's speaking! The big boy's saying something!'

I did have a couple of friends but even they began to distance themselves from me. Fair weather friends, I suppose they were. They weren't strong enough to stand up for me because they knew it would turn bad for them if they did.

I forced myself to go to school each day and tried to close my ears to what the other kids said about me. Surely, I thought, when I moved school – when I went up to secondary school – it would be a new start and all this crap would stop?

But I was wrong.

I didn't think that the bullying, the name-calling and all the rest could possibly get any worse, but it was at secondary school that it got really bad. There was much more physical stuff at secondary school.

At home I began to have nightmares about what they'd do to me the next day and every single morning it would be a huge effort to make myself get out of bed, knowing what lay ahead.

Slowly, miserably, I would get dressed and ready for school; I'd sometimes have trouble keeping my breakfast down. My stomach would clench with dread and my head would buzz. And the nearer I got to the school gates, the worse it became.

I had to force myself, step by step, to keep going forward, my heart pounding against my ribs, my breath coming in short gasps and make myself go through those gates again, day after day, knowing exactly what I was in for when I reached the form room.

I'd walk towards the form room, dragging my feet, going as slowly as I could. If the door was closed, I'd have a moment's grace, a moment to gather myself together, to psych myself up for what was to follow. If the door was open I'd have no time to prepare; I'd have to walk straight into the lion's den.

Every morning, before the teacher arrived, I knew what would happen. They'd be waiting for me; it didn't matter who was there, whether there were only a few of them or if they were all there. They all joined in with the game.

Whizz … thud.

Something would fly through the air, aimed at my head.

I'd duck. Sometimes it hit me, sometimes it missed.

I'd blink and shamble forward towards my seat.

I never wanted to get to my seat because once I was there I was a sitting target. But what else could I do?

They'd pick up their weapons then. Anything that came to hand – long rulers, chairs, whatever – and hit me with them. Slap, slap, punch, punch, poke, poke. I'd put my head down on my desk and cover it with my hands while it was going on, praying for the teacher to come in and put a stop to the torture.

And all this physical stuff was accompanied by the taunts; usually about my size but sometimes other personal comments, too, really hurtful things.

'Lard arse!'

'Boffin!'

'Ape!'

At break and at lunchtime I was always excluded. I tried to stay well out of the way of my tormentors but they were everywhere and whenever I walked past them they would lash out at me.

A pinch here. A punch there. Grabbing my clothes, pulling my hair.

Always accompanied by the same old taunts and insults.

I was sent to Coventry; no one would talk to me and if they did then they'd get into trouble from the others.

If I could, I'd hide away at break times and find a quiet corner where no one would see me. But there aren't many quiet corners in a school. Sooner or later they'd flush me out.

'Found you! Look at him, hiding away like a big baby!'

Then, so long as they were out of sight of the cameras, they'd start chucking stuff at me again. Clods of earth – anything they could pick up.

Some of the worst things happened when we had to shower after games. I was really self-conscious about my body and I hated stripping off.

All their eyes would be on me, smirking, waiting for me to undress.

'Look at him. He's gross!'

They'd pick up their weapons then. Anything that came to hand – long rulers, chairs, whatever – and hit me with them.

They'd all laugh at my body and slap me about. Flicking wet towels at me was one of their favourite games. And I even had pins stuck in me.

You can imagine how I dreaded the days we had games.

Day after day, week after week, year after year, these horrible things happened to me. Sometimes my tormenters would lose interest in me for a bit, but then it would all start up again.

It never let up. They'd dream up new insults – verbal and physical.

I'd been a bright student – once – but not any more. I was so tense and scared that I couldn't think properly and my work really suffered. I could hardly write I was so scared and I could only concentrate on how to get through each day. Every day was a day to be endured, never enjoyed.

My school report said: 'Zac has difficulty mixing'.

Difficulty mixing! When I was younger I'd had no difficulty mixing. But there was no point in trying to mix now. If I'd tried to mix I'd have been in even worse shit!

The school didn't know the half of it!

Mum and Dad were worried about me; I wasn't talking much at home. I was becoming withdrawn and putting on more weight because food was one of the few things that comforted me. I did tell them that kids at school were being mean to me but I never told them how bad it was.

My parents went into the school several times to talk to the teachers about the bullying but the problem was never solved. Sometimes the ringleaders were excluded for a day but then that made things even worse for me. As soon as they came back, the taunts would redouble:

'Snitch.'

'Sneak.'

'Grass.'

My nightmares about school got really scary and I'd wake up sweating with fright, just at the moment when someone was about to knife me or put my head down the toilet.

What with no decent sleep and all the stuff I was going through every day, I started to get ill. I had this persistent dry chesty cough that wouldn't go away. At the time I didn't realize it, but the cough was my brain's way of telling my body that I wasn't coping any longer; that I had had enough.

Being sick was a way of avoiding going to school, of avoiding the hell that awaited me there.

I started to have days – then weeks – off school. I would sit alone at home staring into space, numb to everything.

Even though I was at home, away from my tormenters, I could never relax, never do anything. Just sit in a sort of stupor. And the nightmares didn't stop. I knew that, sooner or later, I'd have to go back and face the bullying. And then they'd have a real go at me for being away. Depriving them of their sick pleasure.

It was after one of the periods of being off school when my cough had cleared up and I knew I'd have to go in again, that I finally flipped.

All night I'd been awake, thinking of the day ahead, dreading going back to school, knowing how bad it would be.

When the morning came I crawled out of bed, but I didn't get any further.

'I've got to get up,' I told myself. 'I've got to get ready for school.'

But my body wouldn't obey. I sat on my bed, not moving. Unable to force myself to do anything.

Dad called me several times. Eventually he came into my room: 'Come on, son, it's time for school. Get dressed. You're going to be late.'

I stared at him. I hardly understood what he was saying. Something had suddenly snapped inside me and I knew that I had reached the end of my tether.

He kept repeating the words and eventually they penetrated my brain and I reacted.

'No!' I yelled at last. 'No! I can't go back. I can't go to school. I'm never going to go to that place again.'

I broke down completely and started sobbing then and gradually – very gradually, over the following days and weeks – I told them the truth about what had been happening to me all those years.

My parents were terribly upset. Horrified at what I told them. They had no idea how bad things had become at school. No idea how long my torture had been going on.

But once they realized how serious it was and how it had affected me, they were brilliant. They promised me that I wouldn't have to go back – ever – and my mum gave up her job to look after me at home, even having me sleep in with her so she could comfort me when the nightmares were so bad.

For the next two years I was in a really dark place. So dark that I don't really remember too much about it. I was like a zombie; I never left the house without one of my parents, but I hardly spoke to them – or to my brothers – and I know they felt desperate that they couldn't reach me.

I felt that I was completely worthless and that everyone would be better off without me, but my mum was there for me, day in, day out, and I knew she wouldn't give up trying to bring me back from where I was to some sort of normal life.

During this period I did have some fantastic help from a doctor who really understood what had happened to me; a specialist in helping young people who had been through difficult times and talking to this doctor really made a difference and started letting in a chink of light and making me think that perhaps, in the future, I could enjoy myself again, think again, work again. I also had a lot of help from a counsellor who talked me through ways of dealing with my feelings.

The medication the doctor gave me was a help too, and I'm still on it.

There was only one letter from the school after I left and then nothing. The local authority sent a letter, too, but there was no follow up.

I was a nobody. I had slipped through the net and no one cared.

Except my family. My two brothers did their best to help but by that stage I could hardly communicate and I know they found me difficult. But my parents always supported me although it must have been horrible for them to see me in such a state and to get so little response from me.

Then one day my mum read about Red Balloon in a magazine. The article said that they were starting up a Red Balloon school in our town and would like any interested people to go along to a meeting.

Well, Mum and Dad went along to the meeting. They met Carrie and heard what Red Balloon was doing – *and* they met other parents of bullied children.

That was a turning point.

I was really reluctant to go to any school at all but finally I was persuaded to at least go and find out about what they were doing.

There was no school building then, just a church hall. And only five students, all beginning together.

So I decided to give it a go.

At first I was really scared. I'd done no school work for two years; I had difficulty in communicating with other people, even my family. And I found it hard to concentrate, or even to read and write.

But everyone was really encouraging and let me go at my own pace, so – slowly – I started to relax and make progress. It was a relief, too, to be with kids who had been through the same stuff as I had – some had had an even worse time – and gradually we learned to trust each other, and the staff.

Coming from the horrible place where I'd been, mentally, I can hardly believe that I'm at college now, doing a course I really enjoy and being able to interact with other students.

Slowly I regained some confidence and some enjoyment of life.

It didn't happen overnight. It happened bit by bit, the growth in self-confidence, self-belief, and I'm not saying that I don't still have down days. I have flashbacks, too, sometimes, though these are getting fewer.

But Red Balloon gave me back a life. It's not the life I had before all the bullying started – that confident, happy boy has gone for ever; I'm not who I was then and I never will be – but at least I have a future now.

ZAC'S DAD

Zac's dad just thought that Zac wasn't enjoying school much and his attitude was that kids can be mean to each other but you get over it. And he says that he was always pushing Zac, wanting him to achieve.

He bitterly regrets that he didn't pick up on the depth of Zac's misery. Neither he nor Zac's mum had any idea how bad things were. They both went to the school to talk about the fact that Zac was being picked on and were reassured that it would be dealt with; they assumed that this would happen and that the whole thing would blow over.

Peter, Zac's dad, comes over as a confident man but he himself admits that when he realized how (in his view) he had failed his son, his own self-confidence took a massive blow. Neither he nor his wife saw the breakdown coming so when it happened it was a huge shock to the whole family.

'What really scared me wasn't so much his sobbing but the fact that Zac didn't seem able to move, except to rock, to and fro, to and fro. I realized then that he was in serious trouble.'

They acted quickly, and immediately contacted a local mental health clinic where Zac received excellent medical and psychological help. This help, together, later, with Red Balloon's unique way of teaching and recovery methods, has brought their son back to them, but those two years locked in his own world at home were a terrible time, a constant worry about Zac's state of mind. It got so bad sometimes, and Zac's self-esteem was so low, that he contemplated taking his own life.

Peter says that when he and his wife went to hear about Red Balloon and met up with other parents whose children had been bullied, the relief was immense. Here was a safe place to learn and teachers who really understood what bullied kids had been through.

'For the first time we realized that we weren't alone,' he said. 'There were other parents there. Parents who were as desperate and confused as us. I don't think that there was one person, during that first evening, who didn't break down in tears, partly because they were hearing about the misery of other children, but partly, too from the huge relief that here was a glimmer of light at the end of a very dark tunnel.'

COMMENTS FROM RED BALLOON STAFF

I have on my study wall a picture of a kingfisher which Zac drew for me in his last year at Red Balloon. Its fine detail and bright colours remind me of the person who travelled a long way in the three years he spent at Red Balloon. I have memories of Zac concentrating on a series of beautiful bird pictures. I have memories of his face lit up with laughter at some obscure joke that appealed to his individual sense of humour. I have memories of Zac performing in the Christmas pantomime. I have memories of Zac sharing ideas, thinking about problems of others in the group and giving advice. I have many memories of Zac cooking and feeding the group. Overall, they are memories of someone emerging into the light.

Zac was one of the founder members of the Red Balloon group in our town. We started as a centre for voluntary students and volunteer teachers four years ago. Everyone was there because they wanted to be there. I recall Zac's nervousness as we started up and how withdrawn he was. He struck me as a very fragile person although at that stage I had no idea of the extent of the bullying he had received or the damage it had done to him. I started to realize this when we talked about the work he wanted to do at Red Balloon and I then found someone who was absolutely paralysed. It was clear that he was an able student but he was unable to engage in relatively simple tasks. It seemed to me that there was 'white noise' in his head which really damaged his concentration and confidence. It became apparent that Zac needed a lot of time and space to recover.

The group began to settle down together, five students and five teachers and Zac began to find his place in the group. The formality and courtesy that was developed within the group came naturally to him and he began to adopt the role of the older brother or wise counsellor. He is a thoughtful person and he responded well to the new freedoms and the security that the Red Balloon philosophy provides. Being with other students who had experienced bullying enabled him to view his own experiences in perspective.

Zac's interest in cooking was one of the cornerstones of his recovery. It helped him in several ways. At times the kitchen was a sanctuary to which he could escape, it helped him develop a positive image of himself as a chef and by cooking for us he found a role he was comfortable with within the group. By cooking for us he was able to give and therefore not always see himself as a recipient.

Zac's journey was not all plain sailing. It is hard to overestimate the damage that bullying can do and Zac's time at Red Balloon illustrates how hard it is to overcome such damage. He was prone to bouts of depression which caused him to withdraw from us from time to time. But he always came back. He went through many of the ups and downs of a normal adolescence: experiences that were harder for him to cope with than for many teenagers.

Gradually, over the three years I worked with Zac, a very likeable young man began to emerge. He is reflective, with a dry sense of humour, he can tolerate the irritations of group working and he has the capacity to develop and nurture friendships. His recovery is not complete. He did not, during his time at Red Balloon, regain his academic confidence. I hope that one day he will recover the ability to study and to enjoy the satisfactions of academic learning.

His last contribution at Red Balloon was generous. He planned, cooked and served a three-course meal to the staff here. He recruited help from other students and the detail and care that went into the meal were exceptional. All the staff were touched by the gesture that this meal represented.

I have since seen Zac many times since he left. He returns to Red Balloon frequently to visit us. He is studying at college developing his skills on a catering course. We caught up with him on work experience in a city restaurant. He was a confident and valued member of the team working in the kitchen. He did not look like anyone's victim but like his own person.

DISCUSSION

Carrie Herbert

For some children the constant fear of being beaten up *again,* of being humiliated in front of your peers *again,* of enduring the pain of being on your own at school waiting for someone to pounce, being isolated or ridiculed for another six long hours, the burden of believing that you have let your parents down, the silence that pervades the insidious behaviour, the fact that teachers ignore it, describe it as something else or blame the bullied child for 'asking for it' can have terrible consequences for the family as well as the child.

Over 50 per cent of the children that we have at Red Balloon have seriously contemplated or attempted suicide. Certainly many attempts are simply cries for help because as a consequence of the continual rejection by their peers they suspect there is no end to the torture they suffer and no one will listen to them. But for some their attempts are serious as they feel that death would be an easier option.

Of course as adults we can put this situation into perspective. At most, if it cannot be stopped in school, bullying has a finite life; the bullying may continue until the child finishes compulsory education at 16 and then it is over as he or she moves on to do something else.

However, the child cannot see the situation or the bullying as finite – they see it as lasting for ever.

The consequences of bullying that we have had to deal with at Red Balloon range from attempted suicide through to depression, hiding under the duvet at home and refusing to go out as well as the psychological consequences – self-harm, anorexia, bulimia, panic attacks and flashbacks. And it is not always recognized that severe physical or mental breakdown can also result from bullying.

The effect of bullying on families

For some children their embarrassment at being bullied and the shame they believe it will bring upon them and their family is enough to keep them absolutely silent about their problem. Of course it may also be the case that they do not recognize this behaviour as bullying – seeing bullying as something that happens to other children.

Which means that if a child has a physical and or mental breakdown it will come as an enormous shock to their family. One day seemingly they are all right – albeit quiet, moody, lethargic (is this typical teenage behaviour?) and the next shaking uncontrollably, crying and virtually paralysed by the pain, fear and guilt they have been carrying for weeks, months and, in some cases, years.

For parents this is devastating as they believe that they should have seen the problem coming, should have asked more questions, should have been to see the teachers more often. They have failed to protect their child and they blame themselves.

However, it is essential to move on from this self-blame – and the sooner the better. Finding help, probably of a psychological nature (i.e. counselling or therapy for all concerned: the parents, the bullied child and other siblings) is a route that may help. Coming to understand one's own pain and at the same time dealing with the emotions of guilt, anger, sadness, etc. can help people recover. For that is what the whole family will need to do – recover from the experience.

WHAT WE DO AT RED BALLOON

In our work with recovery, Red Balloon offers parents the opportunity to join a group where they can talk about some of these feelings. Zac's dad spoke of the relief of finding a group of people who shared his experience, who talked the same language of bullying. We have found that these groups are reassuringly positive for the parents who attend them. Led by the centre's coordinator they also cover other aspects of dealing with teenage behaviour and issues such as the overuse of computers, eating disorders, bedtimes and pocket money.

WHAT TEACHERS AND PARENTS/CARERS CAN DO

Children who are happy with friends and confident in their learning at school should have a skip in their step, a twinkle in their eyes and a song in their heart. Does this sound too Pollyanna-ish? Well, maybe it does, but it is the spirit of what I am saying that is important.

For a child who has been systematically bullied over a period of time their skip stops, their twinkle dies and their song goes flat. Of course it does not happen overnight and with a child who is approaching adolescence it is sometimes difficult to interpret whether their grunt in the morning is 'normal teenage behaviour' or depression.

Talking to and discussing feelings with children is an essential part of a parent's work! Circle Time, as has already been discussed, is one way that a teacher can find out to what extent a child is unhappy, depressed or the constant victim of bullying.

Body language is a give away too. Hunched shoulders, crossed arms, no eye contact, quiet voice, unwillingness to get involved with activities that they were happy to be involved in before.

For some parents a school nurse may be able to help – for others it will be the GP. Wherever you go as a parent for help think about how you child has changed. How were they behaving last month, last year, last Christmas? Comparing what they are like now with how they were before may help you decide if you need to get some professional help. Once an appointment has been made, describing how your son/daughter has changed will enable the professional to take a view on what is happening.

7

Vicky's Story

Vicky was 15 at the time of the interview.

> 'The bullying went on in lessons, too. In history, once, a boy cut my hair and someone poured glue on my jumper. And in science they threw paper at me.'

I had no problems at primary school. I loved it there and I was a happy and confident little girl, with lots of friends. There was a whole group of us and we were always in and out of each other's houses. And I did OK at lessons, too.

But when the time came to move schools, not many of my group went on to the same secondary school – only a handful – and that's when the trouble started.

At first, it was OK. In Year 7 I made a new group of friends and everyone seemed to like me.

But then, in Year 8, things started to go wrong. In Year 8 I became best friends with Claire. I got really friendly with her and we started to do everything together.

The trouble was that Claire had another friend called Gemma and Gemma was really jealous. She wanted to be Claire's best friend and she hated Claire spending so much time with me. To begin with she just gave me death stares and wouldn't talk to me but then, when she saw that Claire wasn't going to drop me, she started getting really vicious and spreading horrible, malicious rumours about me.

I would see her whispering to groups of girls and I knew what she was saying because gradually it all trickled back to me the way things do in school. This was the sort of thing she said.

'You want to watch your stuff. That Vicky's a right little thief. She'll nick anything.'

'You don't want to trust Vicky. Don't tell her anything. She'll snitch on you. She'll go behind your back.'

'Have you seen the way she talks to the boys. She's just a tart.'

It wasn't long before the other kids started looking at me differently, with blank faces and ignoring me if I spoke to them or walking away when I came towards them.

At first it was only the girls, but then even the boys started to believe the rumours and turn away from me and that really upset me. I'd always treated boys just the same as my girl friends – they were just mates – and now Gemma was calling me a tart because I was friendly with them. It was horrible.

Poor Claire was stuck in the middle. She still tried to be friends with me and with Gemma, too, but then, as the name-calling got worse and the gang of girls mocking me got bigger, even Claire deserted me.

I couldn't believe it. I'd suggest she came round mine after school, for instance, and she'd freeze me out. The excuses were pretty lame.

'Sorry, Vicky, I can't. My mum wants me at home.'

She'd pick at her jumper while she spoke and never look me in the eyes. I knew it was a lie.

I didn't push it because I understood why she was doing it. It's hard to be friends with someone everyone else hates. Perhaps she'd even come to believe some of the rumours about me.

But it really hurt. We'd been so close and had so much fun together. Even now, I can remember the shock, the sense of betrayal I felt, when I realized that even she was turning against me. That first time when I suggested we do something together and she wriggled out of it, I knew immediately what was happening and this horrible numb feeling went through me.

I regretted, then, that she knew so much about me. Would she join in with the others and laugh at me and taunt me? Would she let on to them all the things I told her in confidence? Would she tell them all my secrets?

I've always had a good sense of humour and to begin with I tried to laugh it off, make a joke of it, although inside I was feeling miserable. Surely they'd soon be bored with getting at me?

But it didn't stop and, as time went on, it got so bad that there was no way I could laugh it off. The constant taunting and name-calling went on every day.

My sense of humour deserted me. I couldn't stand up to them any longer – there were just too many of them. Gradually the size of the gang grew and the taunting got more and more horrible. Really nasty stuff.

'Look at the way the tart walks,' they'd say. And then they'd mince round doing a stupid exaggerated walk.

They'd mock everything about me. My hair, my clothes – even my family.

'Have you seen the tart's mum? Yuk!' And they'd make vomiting noises.

The bullying went on in lessons, too. In history, once, a boy cut my hair and someone poured glue on my jumper. And in science they threw paper at me.

'She'll tell,' taunted one of the girls. 'She's a crybaby. She'll go running to her mum.'

But I didn't tell. I kept it to myself.

It doesn't take long to puncture your self-confidence, to turn you from someone who is happy and who looks forward to every day into someone who feels miserable and alone and who dreads every day. Getting up in the morning was a real effort. Leaving home, knowing what lay ahead: walking through those school gates so slowly, dragging my feet, my limbs heavy, my eyes on the ground, trying to be blind to the stares and deaf to the whispers and the giggling.

And deaf to the silence of no one talking to me.

Not even the adults spoke to me. I felt as though I was gradually being erased, bit by bit, and turning into an invisible lump of nothing. No one liked me. I had nothing to offer. Everyone was against me.

I wasn't learning anything either. I couldn't. I was too scared of what was going to happen to me at break and lunchtime. I was all frozen up inside. And I never spoke up in class any more for fear of being humiliated. I kept quiet and the teachers ignored me.

I became so withdrawn that they didn't even see me. I was a nobody.

And I stopped doing my homework. When I got home I would look at my exercise books and then push them away. They reminded me of school and school reminded me of the bullies in my class. I hated my books.

Even at home I couldn't get away from the bullying. I hated going online because the gang used the internet to torment me. The cyberbullying was horrible, specially the messaging.

Threats, taunts, abuse.

And the phone calls. Saying vicious things and then cutting out, leaving me standing holding my phone, shaking. And sometimes one of them would phone, all nice, and arrange to meet up with me in town.

To begin with, I thought they meant it. That they were going to include me again, so I'd go to where we'd arranged to meet, thinking I should face them, that it would be worse for me if I didn't go and it would give them new reasons to hate me. And then no one would turn up and I'd be alone, standing looking spare in the middle of town.

I could imagine them, laughing amongst themselves, knowing I'd be hanging around, waiting for them.

Strangers would glance at me in the street. Probably they were wondering what I was doing there, all alone, but by that time I thought that the whole world hated me, that everyone who looked at me saw this empty worthless person and despised me.

For a long time I said nothing to my family about what was happening to me at school, and when, at last, I could stand it no longer and I did let on, it just backfired.

I didn't tell my mum some of the worst stuff, but I did tell my big sister. I asked her not to tell Mum and said I'd sort it out, but she was so worried about me that she went straight to Mum and told her. And Mum went straight to the year head.

Big mistake!

We thought the year head would take some action but she said she had to speak to the pupils I was accusing and get their side of the story.

Why? Why didn't she believe me? Why did she have to hear their side? Couldn't she see what was happening to me? Couldn't the teachers see how I was being taunted, being sent to Coventry, day after miserable day?

Of course, when she did speak to the kids I'd accused, they rounded on me and all it did was to make them hate me even more.

'Sneak!'

'Snitch!'

'Cry-baby!'

'Running to your mummy!'

After that, Mum kept asking me if things at school were getting any better and I had to tell her that they weren't so she kept on phoning the school, but whenever she complained about how I was treated, it just seemed to make things even worse. It always got back to my tormenters.

'You're just a sneaking little grass, Vicky! We all hate you!'

Eventually, I moved forms and for a while the bullying stopped. It was such a relief – but it didn't last long and it seemed that the kids were just waiting to pounce on me again. It all started up again when I fell out with a friend and she turned on me. It was the Claire scenario with a twist.

I moved form again but this time it made no difference. By this time I was a target and whichever form I was in, the bullying continued.

Mum and Dad thought of sending me to a different school but I knew that wouldn't work. The trouble was that the gang of girls at my school – the ones who did most of the bullying – were all part of a wider gang in the town where I live and there were members of the town gang at all three of the local secondary schools. If I'd moved schools, there would have been plenty of people who knew about me and believed the rumours spread about me. The bullying would have continued wherever I went.

It was relentless. It never stopped. Day after day after day, week after week. When it had been going on for two and a half years there was a horrible incident in the summer term when I was attacked by a group of about 20 kids.

It took four teachers to break it up!

I think that this was when I started to crack up. I remember punching the wall, again and again, with my knuckles, until they were cut and bleeding, transferring the pain from my messed up head. I was desperate. I would be bullied for the rest of my life. I could see no end to it.

When my parents complained about the incident the staff said it had all started because I had brought some alcohol in to school.

Alcohol!! All I had was an innocent bottle of apple juice! It was so unfair!

Things got even nastier. The gang started to threaten my sister and my brother, too, when they tried to stand up for me. There was one time, in the supermarket, when some gang members had cornered me and were ramming a trolley into me. My big brother went up to them and told them to stop. One of the girls shouted right in his face that I was just an f…ing tart.

My brother saw red! He lost it then and head-butted her.

I was so grateful to him for taking my side, but then things got bad for him, too. As soon as the girl he'd punched found out he was 18, she complained to the police about him. And so my poor brother was cautioned – as if it was his fault!

It wasn't his fault, it was mine. Everything was my fault. I felt guilty all the time. My brother and sister were getting grief because of me and my parents were worried sick.

Once when I was in the house with my sister, some members of the gang came for me. They kept banging on the door and shouting for me to come. I was terrified and hid in my room and made my sister answer the door. They kept asking for me and I was sobbing and shaking.

'Don't let them in! Don't let them get me!'

I remember punching the wall, again and again.

Eventually, my sister got rid of them but by that time, I was in a terrible state. What would happen next time they came? What would happen if I was on my own in the house?

There was nowhere I could be safe from them. Not even in my own home.

It got so bad that it was a real effort to leave the house at all, I was that scared. Specially as one of the gang members lived two doors down from me.

By that time my head was in a real muddle and I started to cut myself – on my arms and on my thighs. Somehow it was some relief from the pain I was feeling inside. I'd lie about the cuts on my arms and say I'd fallen or I'd scraped them, but Mum knew something was really wrong.

I hated myself, I hated my life and even though my family were really caring, I started to hate them, too. I didn't believe they loved me; nobody could love me, I was so horrible.

I didn't know myself any more; the happy girl I had been had vanished. My personality had completely changed. I would scream and shout abuse at my family and slam doors round the house. Poor things, they tried to get through to me, tried to help me, but I was beyond help. Nothing could cure my pain and I really, really wanted it to end.

I wanted the pain to end. I wanted my life to end. I couldn't see any way out of the nightmare and I didn't want to live any more.

I reached breaking point around Christmas. It was a horrible time. I was out of control. My head was messed up. I couldn't think. All I could do was shout and scream at anyone who came near me. I was like a wild animal, lashing out. A caged wild animal with nowhere to turn.

I remember standing in the hall, yelling and punching the wall – I often punched the wall until my knuckles bled – when suddenly my dad came up to me. He's a big strong bloke and even though I was lashing out he managed to pick me up. He carried me upstairs to my room, still screaming and thrashing about and kicking, and just sat with me. Gradually I calmed down.

He didn't leave. He just waited. And at last he got me to talk to him. To open up about what was happening. It took a long time and he was very patient. He listened and occasionally asked questions. We sat up in my bedroom and talked for three hours.

When he went downstairs I heard him talking to Mum and sobbing.

'How could they do that to her? How could they treat my little girl like that?'

It went on and on and my mum was comforting him. It was really frightening. I'd never heard my dad cry before. I never realized that he could crumple up like that.

But they both realized then that something had to be done. I couldn't go on as I was and they couldn't force me to go back to school after the holidays.

They were as desperate as I was. They didn't know where to turn – and nor did I.

It was the most miserable Christmas of my life.

Then, just after Christmas, Mum saw a programme on the telly about Red Balloon. How lucky was that? I don't know what would have happened to me if she'd not seen it.

She emailed them immediately to ask if they could help us and, 20 minutes later, Carrie Herbert was on the phone, telling her all about Red Balloon and inviting us to come and visit the Learner Centre in Cambridge.

Mum said she knew it was the place for me as soon as we walked through the door. It's quite different from a school. It's in a house and it's like being part of a big family.

He just sat with me. Gradually I calmed down.

I started there in the January. It's such a relief. All the kids at Red Balloon have been through the same sort of stuff as me. Some of them have had an even worse time.

There's no bullying at Red Balloon and everyone cares about you. I feel like a person again and at last I am able to relax. People notice me and talk to me – the students and the staff – and any worries or concerns are aired right away. My mind has begun to unfreeze and I can study again. I no longer feel I'm rubbish at everything, that I'm worthless; there are things I *can* do – even things I'm good at – and I'm going to take my GCSEs next year.

At first when I went back on the train to my home town in the evenings, my stomach would clench up with anxiety when I walked back from the station, and I'd be looking over my shoulder all the time, jumping at any little noise, thinking the gang would still be watching out for me. But it hasn't happened. I suppose that now I'm away from them they've lost interest in me. Out of sight, out of mind. Perhaps they've found some other poor girl to torture.

I used to love singing and dancing – especially tap and ballet – and I performed in London with my dance school when I was younger, but when I hated myself so much I lost confidence in my ability to do anything – let alone dance and sing. I thought I was no good. How could I be any good?

Now I'm beginning to feel like dancing and singing again.

COMMENTS FROM RED BALLOON STAFF

Now that she is in a safe environment, Vicky is visibly relaxing. She is learning to play the guitar and she is beginning to show good organizational skills. She also delighted us with her dancing recently when she took part in a workshop given by our students at local primary schools during anti-bullying week to demonstrate feelings experienced by bullied children.

Her dancing was genuinely exceptional and gave her an opportunity to shine in the presence of her peers.

She has contributed to the life of Red Balloon in other ways, too. She helped to present a fellow student's work at a recent fundraising event, she performed in the school play and joined in our 'Outward Bound' week away in the Lake District. She has also helped other students to enjoy dance.

Vicky would be an asset to any course of education that valued practical energy, good personal skills and academic ability. She has overcome external difficulties with determination and diligence. She has recovered the confidence to join in and contribute to community life and to work steadily, as she has done on various academic projects, to achieve her goals.

Vicky is getting stronger and more assertive all the time; this is demonstrated by a recent incident where she stopped a fellow student from self-harming by calmly removing a knife from him and reassuring him. She is a caring girl and looks after other students when they need help.

Here are some of the comments in her achievement record:

'Vicky, it has been lovely to see you finding your feet within group sessions, especially in citizenship, where you are starting to express your own views and question the views of other people…You have been a member of the school band this year, and have done extremely well at picking up chords quickly… I know you'll hate me for this, but you really do have a lovely singing voice!'

'I have been very impressed by your response to our 20th Century play. Not only did you appreciate the professional production at the theatre but you also read and commented in group readings with flair and insight.'

'Vicky, I think you're really good at looking at poetry. You notice little details and enjoy the humour, too. You are beautifully open to what the writers are telling us, and happy to talk about what you feel is going on. You absorb new words really well, and have a very good memory.'

'It has been excellent to have you amongst us at the heart of the social life here: you have become very important to us all. You are warm and open and lively.'

'When you open up you are a powerhouse!'

DISCUSSION

Carrie Herbert

Children can be bullied in a variety of ways and in this case the method used against Vicky was rumour-mongering, gossiping, spreading lies, and cyber-bullying as well as using physical attacks and threatened attacks to the family and the home itself.

Cyber-bullying is clearly a recent innovation. Thirty years ago words were scribbled in indelible pens on the back of loo doors or daubed on the bike sheds and on walls and fences near to the school. This still goes on, of course, but bullying using the written word has now moved on to another level.

One of the unpleasant attributes of graffiti is the anonymity of the attacker. 'Susie Blogs is a slag' whilst not only unkind, untrue and a personal attack masks the identity of the person saying/doing/thinking it. At least being called a slag to your face lets you know who the enemy is. Wall-writing makes you fearful as to who the perpetrator might be and at the same time allows the writer to get away with it. Unless their writing can be identified they remain hidden, having written it alone, in the cubicle out of sight. This can make children who bully in this way feel very powerful.

Cyber-bullying

To some extent cyber-bullying has similar attributes to wall-writing. And let's be clear how many ways bullying can happen in cyberspace: text messages, MSN messages, emails, Twitter and social networking pages such as Facebook.

Some of these messages can be sent whilst the identity of the sender can be omitted. Thus a message saying 'You are a slag' can be sent to the recipient without the recipient knowing who is behind it. However, not only is the identity hidden, these messages can come tripping into a child's phone or onto the computer anytime during the day, evening and at night too. Children who are alone, have few friends or are miserable are often desperate for a text message or email – and therefore leave their phones and computers on.

Sending unpleasant messages to a target is clearly bullying, but cyber-bullying can get far worse.

While comments like 'no one likes you', 'you are the ugliest girl in the school', 'your mum is a whore' can be damaging there are other ways to intimidate and frighten. Threats to a child's safety; 'We are going to beat you up', 'stab you' and even 'we will kill you' are messages that should be taken seriously and given to the police. These go beyond bullying and are threats of actual physical violence.

WHAT TEACHERS AND PARENTS/CARERS CAN DO

Parents and teachers may be forgiven for believing that cyber-bullying is one of those issues for which there is a very simple solution: turn your phone off, delete unwanted emails from your computer without reading them and don't give everyone at school your number or your email address.

Of course as people over the age of 30 we are 'tourists' to this electronic age, not 'natives'. To not have a phone on, to be unable to be contacted 24/7 is something that spells disaster to most young people – it says something about their likeability, their popularity, their availability. So if turning the machines off is not a possibility it means that we as parents and teachers need to find other ways of helping young people protect themselves from unwanted calls, threatening texts, unpleasant images, or breaches of confidences from one 'friend' to another.

We have to start when the child is young, talking about the way in which people communicate. This of course is not new. Speaking politely, with respect, letting others talk, and listening to each other are all skills that we want and expect young people to have. But in the past much of this was learned 'on the hoof', as they grew up. However, some children today have to be taught these skills.

And along with communication skills comes their self-belief. Talked about in other chapters, a child's self-confidence and their self-belief that they can do what they set out to do, by not putting them down, but by having realistic expectations, helping them manage their expectation and not believe they are invincible are ways in which children can find out how the world works and their place in it.

Clearly the communication that is the most important and is at the heart of this type of bullying is the ability for children to be able to talk to their parents or carers. If and when things do get out of hand, when communication goes sour on the internet, in whatever form, children need to know that their parents can help them deal with it and they are not alone.

Threats of violence and threats 'to kill' or 'beat up' a child at school need to be taken seriously and on occasions the police will need to be involved.

Friendships that go wrong

Friendships that go wrong have often been the source of ammunition for people who wish to wreck another's happiness. Secrets told in confidence to each other at the height of a friendship can all too easily be revealed when the friendship dissolves.

However, cyber-bullying takes this to another level. Consensual photos taken of oneself or another person in jest or love or friendship in one situation can become compromising information, evidence of illegal activity or indiscreet behaviour at the touch of a button within seconds. Suddenly what was once private and personal between two people has worldwide distribution.

If one's family is threatened and the family home attacked it follows that the target would blame themselves for the way the bullying has leached into family life. That is one of the reasons why children keep quiet and do not tell their parents. By telling, the situation can become exacerbated if those that are told use force, threat or punishment against those doing the bullying.

WHAT WE DO AT RED BALLOON

At Red Balloon we use a variety of ways to encourage children and young people to look at their behaviour – both good and bad behaviour – and to understand the emotions linked with it. Restorative justice lies at the heart of much of the work we do, making sure those who have been hurt have a voice and that those who did the hurting can hear the pain in the recipient's voice and understand the impact their behaviour had. At Red Balloon we use restorative justice as a tool for making sure both children involved in an incident, whether the target or the aggressor, understand the feelings, reasons for behaving that way, issues that both parties may have, or the purpose behind the behaviour of the other person.

Restorative justice is an approach to justice that focuses on the needs of victims and offenders, instead of the need to satisfy the abstract principles of law or the need of the community to exact punishment. Victims are given an active role in a dispute and offenders are encouraged to take responsibility for their actions, 'to repair the harm they've done – by apologising, returning stolen money, or (for example) doing community service.'[1] It is based on a theory of justice that focuses on crime and wrong doing as acted against the individual or community rather than the state. In restorative justice processes the justice system has the person who has done harm and the person who has been harmed take an active role. The victim may receive an apology, direct reparation or indirect action to restore or fix the damage. Restorative justice can involve a fostering of dialogue between the offender and the victim showing the highest rates of victim satisfaction, true accountability by the offender, and reduced recidivism.

At Red Balloon if there is an incident between two children, and on occasions there is, we use the method for dealing with it as a learning opportunity. In the case of sorting out the incident using restorative justice both parties are allowed to talk about what they think happened, what was intended, where they feel they made a mistake, how they would play it differently now, to take responsibility for things they said or did and to make appropriate reparation if damage, hurt or upset was caused. It is essentially a no-blame approach but one where children understand if they have been responsible for upset.

WHAT TEACHERS AND PARENTS/CARERS CAN DO

There is much pressure by society to punish the children responsible for bullying but in many cases this method fails and does exactly the opposite of what is required. Swedish academic Dan Olweus pioneered a programme where those who are the aggressors are dealt with in a respectful and educative way, raising their level of understanding so that they are encouraged to have empathy for and to recognize the impact their behaviour might have had on their target. By educating those who use bullying tactics aggressive acts can be reduced. The target is not further taunted and bullied and the teachers can expect a better chance of restoring equilibrium than by using punishment.

1 Webber, R. (2009) 'A new kind of criminal justice.' *Parade, 29* October 2009. Available at www.parade.com/news/intelligence-report/archive/091025-a-new-kind-of-criminal-justice.html, accessed 6 December 2010.

It is clear from the stories we have recorded that bullying and unpleasant behaviour happens in many classrooms under the noses of the teachers teaching. How can this be? Why do the teachers not realize that all is not well with the health of the classroom? Battling to teach against rival power bases, the teacher versus a gang of aggressors versus a single target does not make for effective learning.

How much better it would be if the teacher stopped the class, got all the children in a circle and began a Circle Time, saying, for instance: 'I know that there are competing factions in this lesson and I am sure that not everyone is happy with this. I am also sure that not everyone is involved. I suggest we start by going round the circle and each person describe what they think the feelings are in the room at the moment. Can we start with you John?' (Choosing a child who is unlikely to be involved.)

Teaching against a mood of unrest, petty squabbling and bullying does not help with the learning. Whatever time it takes to sort out the competing factions is time gained in the long term for effective learning.

It would be unreasonable to expect every teacher to feel competent to deal with such an issue as unrest in the classroom and to be able to ditch their lesson plan and manage an unstructured session in which children are encouraged to discuss their feelings, to explain and articulate what has happened and to make decisions and plans for a better classroom atmosphere. If you feel that you are in this situation it is important to find another member of staff who can help you do this. Maybe someone from the Personal and Social Education (PSE) pastoral team could lead such a session and you could watch and learn. To ignore these conflicting emotions within the class is to store up trouble for the future and to expect them to be resolved of their own accord is unrealistic.

8

Cameron's Story

Cameron was 15 at the time of the interview.

> 'That's all I've ever wanted. Just to be allowed to be myself and to act in a way that seems natural to me.'

I suppose I've always been different and I'm quite flamboyant, but the really bad, day after day name-calling, sniggering and pushing only began when I started at this special school for boys.

The school's not been going that long and it's for boys with behavioural problems. They come from all over the county and there's room for about 80 pupils; some are day boys and some are weekly boarders. I was a boarder.

My foster parents thought the school would suit me so my foster mum arranged it all. I don't live with either of my birth parents though I do see them three times a year. My real mum has a lot of medical problems and my real dad has mental problems and they couldn't cope with me so I've been fostered since I was two years old. I have three older brothers. Two live with my real dad and the eldest lives with his fiancée. I'm really close to one of my brothers – Sam. He's gay, too, and he understands about all the horrible stuff I've been through.

So, I began at this new school. The school's website made a big deal about keeping pupils safe, showing them respect and valuing them. They said that pupils experienced:

> 'supportive relationships'
>
> 'respect and being valued'

She helped me organize a fashion show.
We had a catwalk and everything.

'positive adult role models'

'a sense of safety and security'.

Well, all this sounded pretty good!

Except that, so far as I was concerned, none of it was true.

I certainly never got much respect. There were only two teachers who ever gave me any respect or made me feel valued. The rest of the staff – and most of the boys – gave me nothing but aggravation.

Here are some of the things they called me:

'Poof.'

'Gayboy.'

'Fairy.'

'Woman.'

There were several other gay and bisexual boys at the school and we formed a group, but for some reason I was the one most of the other boys picked on. Perhaps it was because I stood out more than the rest. It was hard for the other members of my group; mostly, they would drift away when it got bad and I can't say I blame them.

The name-calling and the sniggering never stopped. It happened *every single day* I was at that school, mostly at break and lunchtime.

It wore me down. I pretended that I didn't care but deep down I was really upset and I started to get very depressed.

And as for the school's boast that it was a place of 'safety and security'! Well, I can tell you it certainly wasn't safe. I knew that some of the kids brought in knives and there were hardly any security cameras on the site. I was constantly scared I'd be attacked.

But I was never *badly* attacked. The boys would push me about and the teachers would restrain me when I got gobby with them. Sometimes I'd yell and scream at them because I felt I had to react. The only time I was hit was when I hit a teacher and he hit me right back.

But there were *some* good times at the school. There was this American teacher, Miss B, who really understood me and was my mentor. She was great. She helped me organize a fashion show; we had a catwalk and everything. And she'd got hold of a great meringue-type wedding dress and let me redesign it, which was brilliant. And she put on plays, too, and gave me great parts in them.

And there was another teacher, Mrs C, who was lovely, too. She used to invite me to her house and I was very friendly with her daughter; we'd play computer games together.

But they were the only two teachers who were good to me. The others all gave me grief.

There were some ugly incidents at that school. For example, once a teacher chucked a table at me at lunchtime and pushed me against the dinner counter.

And there was the time when I got very down about the name-calling and the pushing and felt I couldn't stand it no longer so I went to the head and said I was being victimized. The head told me I was fussing and telling tales and that I should stop behaving like a woman.

Great!

Another time, one of the boys reported me to the head saying I was coming on to him, that I fancied him, and he didn't like it – it scared him. It was all nonsense. I didn't fancy him at all. He was just making it up, but it got me in a lot of trouble and after that I felt I was being watched all the time.

I had a best friend – Alex – who was bisexual and his friendship kept me sane. He's still a really good friend. He and I slept in the same dormitory. Sometimes other boys would come in and start whispering together and giggling and pointing at us.

'Look what they're doing.'

'They're disgusting!'

'Perverts.'

In fact, we never did anything sexual. We were just friends who stuck together. Alex had real trouble with the teachers. He had really tiny writing and it was very difficult to read it. The teachers went on and on at him about this and they'd rip his work up in front of him.

It got so bad that Alex even considered committing suicide. I was really worried about him and I hope I supported him; I tried my best. He knew I'd be his friend whatever happened and I think that helped him through the bad times.

Sometimes Alex and I would be so desperate to get out of the place that we'd skive off school. The school was right out in the country and there wasn't much to do but it felt good to be away from the grief we got from the staff and the other boys. Then one day we were spotted by the head and there was big trouble. That put a stop to our little outings and after that, the feeling of being watched – spied on – got worse and worse.

I felt I could hardly breathe without someone checking up on me.

Things went from bad to worse at that school and I'd sort of begun to shut down. I wasn't learning anything – I was too miserable and too busy watching my back. Anyway, the head said I wasn't worth teaching.

When an adult says that to you, you may flounce off and say you don't care, but you do. What little self-esteem you have is punctured like a balloon being deflated. I was already in a pretty bad way – my head was messed up and I didn't like myself much, though I always tried to hang on to some shred of self-respect – and then for someone in authority to tell me, in so many words, that I was worthless! Well, you can imagine how bad that made me feel. I was really low.

Things got worse and worse. I felt that everyone was against me and no one much cared what happened to me. The whole world seemed to hate me. No one understood me. But, even then, when I was feeling so low, I still had a bit of spirit left and if people badmouthed me then I'd still badmouth them right back.

Because of my 'attitude' the school decided to separate me from the other boys and I spent most of Year 11 in the place they called the white room. The white room was where they put boys who they said were disruptive.

Although, in some ways, it was a relief to be on my own, to be away from the constant taunts, in another way it was a really bad time. I had too much time to think about what had happened, to think of why everything was in such a mess. And to wonder what would become of me. After a while I stopped speaking.

What was the point in talking to people? Most of the staff didn't listen anyway and they certainly didn't understand me and most of the pupils mocked me. It was too much effort to keep saying the same things back, over and over, so I stopped saying anything.

I'd look round the white room, focusing on one tiny thing. Maybe a nail or a cobweb or a stain on the wall. I had to, to stop myself slipping down and down, into the deep well that was waiting to drown me, to close over my head.

I did think of giving up completely and for a while I stopped eating. Would anyone care if I weren't around? Would anyone notice?

No one except Alex – and the two teachers I mentioned.

But even though I was feeling so low, even at the very worst time, and even though my self-respect had taken a massive blow, I don't think that I ever lost it completely. I am who I am and I can't change that. The problems come from people not letting me be myself.

That's all I've ever wanted. Just to be allowed to be myself and to act in a way that seems natural to me.

I saw out my time at that school and left at the end of Year 11 – and, although I was counting the days, the hours, the minutes to getting out of the place, to kicking the dust of it from off my feet, I had no idea what I was going to do next.

My social worker helped me though. She was one of the people who didn't let me down. I didn't give her the silent treatment. I did talk to her and I found I could confide in her a bit.

She was the one who told me about Red Balloon.

I must admit, I did feel a flicker of excitement when she described it to me. Maybe, just maybe, here was a place where I could be myself? Could it be a new start for me?

But I'd learnt not to build up my hopes too high. I'd been let down too often. After all, my foster parents had said the other school would be great for me.

When I first looked round Red Balloon, I was really surprised. It didn't seem like a school at all, more like a home with a big family.

I was nervous at first, nervous that, once again, the taunting would start. Taunting with the words I'd heard so often.

'Fairy.'

'Poof.'

'Gayboy.'

'Woman.'

But there was none of that. All the other kids there had been through their own hell. They all knew what it was like to be got at.

The staff there were really supportive, too. For the first time I felt that I was treated as a real person. They all saw beyond my looks, my sexuality, and what they saw was just Cameron. A boy with a lot of problems but with a lot to give, too.

And it was at Red Balloon that I found I could help other people. The other kids would confide in me – tell me some of the stuff they'd been through – and I found it easy to listen to them and support them. It made me feel good about myself. I even began to feel popular!

Gradually I began to get ahead with my work. When you are safe your head unfreezes and you can think. And having one to one lessons really helped me.

But then, while I was at Red Balloon, everything went wrong at home. I'd been with Anne and Dave, my foster parents, for 12 years and I'd been really happy with them. But then they told me that their daughter and her husband and children were coming to live with them too.

The moment they said it, I knew there would be trouble. There was no way it was going to work.

Everything changed when they came. It changed almost as soon as she and her brood walked through the door.

I'd never got on with their daughter and she hated me being in the house with her parents; she said that I was a bad influence on her kids, too.

It seemed to me that she went out of her way to make things hard for me. Although for a lot of the time she just ignored me – sort of pretended I wasn't there and treated me like an annoying bit of furniture – when I dressed up in my high-heeled boots and fancy gear she let rip. Her kids laughed at me and she was really rude.

'You're ridiculous. Don't you realize how stupid you look, all dressed up like that, you nancy boy?'

I gave her the silent treatment, but she went on at me.

'Why are you wearing make-up? It's disgusting!'

Disgusting. Was I really disgusting to other people? I couldn't help what I was. I *liked* wearing make-up. It made me feel good. And I *liked* dressing up.

For all those years I'd been so happy in my foster home. Anne and Dave had been good to me and I'd felt they understood me, accepted me for what I was. They'd always let me dress up and not laughed at me. They'd tried to do the best for me – even sending me to that crap school they'd done with the best intentions because they really felt it would suit me.

But now they were torn two ways and I suppose they felt that they had to support their daughter – their own flesh and blood – even if they could see what she was doing to me.

It got so bad that it was obvious we couldn't both stay in the house and, deep down, I knew I was going to be the one who was kicked out. I knew that it wasn't me who was going to win this battle.

Then one day it all came to a head. I was feeling so upset with her that I just lost it. I don't even remember whether anything particular triggered the screaming match. Maybe it was one taunt too far, maybe it was just a look she gave me. But anyway, suddenly I couldn't take any more and I found myself shouting and ranting at the whole family.

'She hates me!' I yelled, pointing at their daughter.

She didn't answer, just folded her arms.

'Why don't you make her go?' I spluttered. 'I was happy here. I really liked living here until she came along and ruined it all!'

'Calm down, Cameron,' said Dave. 'There's room for all of us here. We've just got to give and take.'

'Give and take? So I've got to do all the taking, have I? I've got to take all the crap she throws at me?'

'Cameron. It's not that bad!'

'It *is*. It *is* that bad.' I was choking on my words, choking with fury and misery. I pointed at her. '*She*'s the problem! She won't accept me for what I am. She *hates* me. She and her precious kids. They laugh at me.'

'Come on, Cameron. No one's laughing at you.'

'They *are*. They're making fun of me. I can't take it. Make her go!'

I couldn't speak for rage and I rushed out of the room, slamming the door behind me and crashed up the stairs to my bedroom.

My bedroom. My sanctuary. How much longer would it be mine?

I sat up there for ages, full of dread, listening to them talking together downstairs. I could hear their daughter's voice, louder than the others. Strident. Insistent. What was she saying about me? What lies was she spreading?

Even though I couldn't hear her words I knew what she was doing. She was poisoning them against me.

And she was successful. She got her way. I was kicked out.

I know that Anne and Dave were sad when they told me they couldn't have me living with them any longer. They knew how unsettling it would be for me, moving from somewhere I'd always felt safe and valued.

Leaving them was horrible.

I remember turning back to look at the house when I left. A place where I'd been settled and happy once.

They were standing at the door, waving. I waved back and tried to look cheerful but inside I was just so churned up with misery.

I was sent to another foster home after that but I hated it. I can't think why I was placed with those people. The man, particularly, just didn't understand me at all.

'Don't think you're wearing make-up in my house,' he screamed at me. 'Go and take it off at once.'

I'd try and sneak out, wearing my stuff, but he was always on the look out for me.

'Come here, you fairy,' he'd shout, and he'd force me to go to my room and get dressed like a 'real boy' and wipe off all my make-up.

I didn't last long there. There were constant rows.

Being unhappy in the foster home really affected my work at Red Balloon and I started to go downhill but I'm in an emergency placement now and it's nice. And my brother Sam is really good to me. I see a lot of him.

I've always felt safe at Red Balloon and I feel at home there. The people there are my family and I've made some really good friends, friends who accept me for who I am.

I have help from a therapist at Red Balloon too. I hate talking about the past and about my family and although our sessions sometimes upset me, they are getting my head straight.

This summer I'm going to do some work experience backstage at the local theatre. And maybe in a hair salon, too. I can't wait.

I've always loved acting and when I leave school I want to get a job involved with the performing arts.

Some people say I look a bit like Gok Wan (the *How to Look Good Naked* bloke) but that's not true!

I just look like me – Cameron – and I enjoy looking the way I do. I love putting on outrageous make-up and high heels and great clothes and showing off to the world!

COMMENTS FROM RED BALLOON STAFF

Cameron had great tenacity and he would see projects through and he could also be a faithful friend. He has a pure heart and if he ever saw anyone in trouble or in pain, he would be the first person to approach them and see if he could help.

He is an emotionally articulate boy and at Red Balloon he was given the time and space to express these emotions in safety – and within boundaries.

Since leaving Red Balloon he has joined a gay support group and has made some new friends and he talks about going to dance classes.

Here are extracts from some of his achievement records:

> 'You are a very warm, kind and sensitive person. The hours we worked together were special and happy ones, full of laughter and also depth: you are someone who can give a lot to others as well as receive.'
>
> 'Your attitude to your work has been mature and sensible and you have taken the entry level tests in your stride and done well in all of them. You have worked hard and definitely deserved your bronze certificate. Well done.'
>
> 'With continued daily practice you'll be a star reader soon!'

And here are some comments that Cameron put in his own report:

> 'I have improved in reading. I now enjoy reading at home. In science I have improved in leaps and bounds. I have enjoyed being in the play. I've helped to get make-up done for the play.'

DISCUSSION

Carrie Herbert

Attention-seeking

Many children like attention. Most children between the ages of three and eight like to be the centre of attention, like to be praised, like to dance, prance and recite in front of guests, family and friends. This is all very normal and part of a child's growing up.

However, usually by the time a child is nearing the teenage years they will have understood that attention needs to be shared, that they cannot have it all the time, that maybe they should only have attention when they have done something especially good, remarkable or brave.

Many of our students like – even demand – attention. If they feel someone else is getting more than their fair share of attention they will begin to 'play up'. This may be by talking louder, laughing more outrageously or tripping up and falling on the floor (all of which could be interpreted as positive in that they feel confident enough to do these things). On the other hand there are the attention-seeking behaviours that are negative: putting others down, crying, getting angry, shoving and pushing, stealing, messing up another person's work or being disruptive in other ways.

WHAT WE DO AT RED BALLOON

At Red Balloon we have staff who are able to handle this. Having seven or eight adults per 15 children (without volunteers) on site at all times means that there is always the opportunity to give attention to the child who wants it. Denying a young person that attention will only make matters worse. Most children, when they are given enough attention, cease to seek it so desperately.

At Red Balloon we have to find out why a young person is seeking attention and there may be many reasons for this. They may need constant reassurance or praise to bolster their fragile self-confidence or they may use attention-seeking to hide their inability to cope academically or to concentrate for any length of time. The reasons for this attention-seeking need to be investigated with the young person and then their problems addressed, on a one to one basis. How long is their attention span, for instance? How can it be prolonged? How are we going to do this? Often, as mentioned before, the answer lies in finding a subject which really engages a child and at which they shine, and building on this. Discussing the way forward with the student and getting them on side is vital.

When a child is constantly disruptive, constantly butting into conversations between a teacher and another student, this can be unsettling for all concerned and the child needs to be aware that this is so. By patiently going over their attention-seeking behaviour with them a teacher can explain why this behaviour disrupts others who are trying to learn and why it is disrespectful not only to staff members but also to their fellow students, reminding them of the Red Balloon ethos of respect for others.

At the same time, it is very important not to stifle natural enthusiasm.

> *Teacher: Charlie, this morning when I was talking to Anna you interrupted me on five different occasions. Once just to show me a paintbrush! And yesterday you interrupted me about six times when I was discussing Jon's work with him. And then at lunchtime today when I was speaking with Edna you kept shaking my arm.*
>
> *Charlie: Yes, but I couldn't find the black paint this morning and yesterday I wanted to show you that I'd finished my model of the castle.*
>
> *Teacher: I am very glad you have finished it and it's a lovely castle but you could have waited until I had stopped talking to Jon.*
>
> *Charlie: I could have but I wanted to get on with the sword I am making.*
>
> *Teacher: I am very pleased that you are eager to get on with the sword but if you had waited until I had finished with Jon then I would have been able to look at your work properly.*

WHAT TEACHERS AND PARENTS/CARERS CAN DO

Some children require more attention than others. In a class of 25+ children this can make life more problematic as three children requiring attention at the same time does not make for an easy lesson. Ignoring children who seek attention is never the way to respond. Asking children to wait, to put their needs on hold and that you will speak to them in five minutes, to write down their problem, to draw their anxiety, to discuss it with another student, to take a walk around the school grounds until you are in a position to deal with their needs are all ways of giving the teacher some time.

For parents it is often easier – purely for the fact that there are fewer children needing attention! Children want attention because they want to feel loved, needed, important, 'special' and all those words that mean they are your son or daughter. It seems to me that if that is what they want why don't we give it to them!

Standing back and analysing when the attention-seeking behaviour starts, why it starts, what has preceded it, or what is coming next can help you build up a picture of the times in your son/daughter's life when they feel your attention is essential. Once you have worked out that they want your attention when another sibling is around, when Grannie is coming to stay, when you have visitors, when you are working and busy, will help you work out strategies to deal with it. Because ignoring it is not the solution.

Speaking with the child explicitly always helps.

'Simon, I know you want my attention. At the moment I am speaking with Grannie, but I will be able to spend time with you in ten minutes. Could you read your book, draw a picture, take the dog in the garden until then?' is saying a number of things:

- I acknowledge that your want attention.
- I will give you attention in ten minutes.
- I am giving someone else attention at the moment.
- You could do something else until I am free – here are some examples.

Once the ten minutes have elapsed it is important to do what you said you would do, even though now they are happily playing with the dog in the garden.

Visiting that 'attention-seeking behaviour moment' and reflecting on it can help the child understand their own behaviour. Helping children understand their own feelings, behaviours and needs, and expressing them appropriately, is a valuable lesson.

On the other hand some children do not know what appropriate behaviour is. Telling children who are playing well together that that behaviour is what you like gives them the knowledge that playing well together is approved of. Always telling children not to do something does not tell them what is right. Praising good, helpful, quiet, diligent, focused behaviour begins to establish what is and what is not appropriate.

Fantasizing

Fantasizing is another form of attention-seeking. Occasionally, children who have been through traumatic experiences can mask reality; there is a gap between who they are and who they want to be and they can compartmentalize information and tell one person one thing and someone else something completely different about their life.

WHAT WE DO AT RED BALLOON

In these cases Red Balloon staff work with the child, getting him or her to accept the person they are – stressing always the positive aspects of their personality and praising their achievements – and encourage them to live in the real world and stop making up stories to build themselves up in the eyes of others, and themselves. Once they begin to realize that they can be respected and liked as the person they really are, then they become more honest with themselves and with others.

Homophobic bullying

Bullying because of one's sexuality is probably one of the hardest forms to deal with. We live in a country where just 50 years ago homosexuality was a criminal activity, where in the late 1980s and early 1990s the government of the day forbade teachers to discuss with their students gay relationships as a positive lifestyle choice, and in the last few decades we have had the scare of Aids, which is still considered by many people to be a 'gay disease'. Even now, in the second decade of the twenty-first century, the church is still debating whether bishops can be gay and whether gay couples should have the right to be 'married' in church before God. There is still so much confusion on this front that it is hardly surprising that gay youngsters find it difficult to 'come out' in schools and colleges.

WHAT WE DO AT RED BALLOON

At Red Balloon we celebrate difference and encourage young people to be comfortable in their own skin, accept who they are and follow their own interests whether these are gender stereotypical or not. All students are taught to respect each other regardless of sexual orientation and helped to understand that this is only one aspect of a student's make up – it does not define him or her. Discussion of homosexuality within boys' and girls' groups is a useful way of exploring this.

WHAT TEACHERS AND PARENTS/CARERS CAN DO

Children test out their sexuality in a variety of ways. For a girl to dress as a boy is often considered to be more appropriate than for a boy to play with dolls. And for many children this is a phase they go through and once explored they are content to have a gender identity that is consistent with their sex.

However, having a gay son or daughter is a reality for many parents and whatever that parent may think, loving them for who they are rather than what they are is the most important thing you can do.

For many young people the years of adolescence are painful anyway. Soaring hormones, rushing ideas, out of control feelings of rage, love and frustration are normal for most teenagers. Adding to that a confusion or anxiety about whether they are gay, what their parents will think, and how they should express their feelings, often leaves them silent, alone and lonely.

Of course homosexuality has not had a particularly good press, as I have already written. The laws against homosexual men in the last century did not encourage people to 'come out' and in fact allowed homophobia to proliferate. Beating up effeminate men, calling them a string of offensive names, has created a society where in some places being gay is a dangerous thing to be. Pop stars and footballers think very hard about how it will affect their fan base before they 'come out'.

So creating an inclusive, open, liberal, accepting atmosphere at home and at school and being able to discuss a range of issues including sexuality is essential. If young gay men and women are to have a place where their views, feelings, needs and concerns are aired, discussed and met along with the concerns and anxieties that all young people have, they have to be part of this too. Discussing gay people in critical, prejudicial and distasteful ways will not only encourage young people to be homophobic but will make those who are thinking they may be gay fear that if they reveal their true identity no one will like them and they will be ostracized. Living a deceitful life where one's feelings have to be controlled, contained, not spoken about and they have to lie is no way for a young person to develop as a young adult in today's world.

PART II

Understanding Bullying Behaviour and Strategies to Prevent It

9

Understanding Bullying Behaviour

Carrie Herbert

As you will have seen in the stories which form the first part of this book, Red Balloon Learner Centres take the issue of bullying very seriously. What is often forgotten is that children who have been bullied know how to bully! So, we run workshops every so often as to what constitutes this behaviour.

Definitions of bullying differ, but the one we use has three conditions.

1. Bullying is any behaviour that is unwanted and unwelcome.
2. It is behaviour that has a negative impact on the recipient or on bystanders.
3. The behaviour is unwarranted.

Having this wide-ranging definition, with clear boundaries, helps children to understand how those at the receiving end might feel as well as why they are justified in feeling the way they do.

The first condition deals with the fact that it is the recipient who decides whether the behaviour is unwanted and unwelcome. The recipient must be in a position to say, 'I find it embarrassing to be called "fatty" or "ginge"' or to be told they can't join a table at lunchtime. Other children in the same position may not have the same feelings.

I came across a book that I was given when I was 11 which says 'To Carrots, love Anne'. At school I was called Carrots, not because I had red hair but because my name was Caroline. I liked my nickname – it meant I belonged, it was a term of endearment and one to which I responded positively. However, had I found it negative and I had been unable to ask them to stop, I would have liked someone to have pointed out to those calling me that name that it was not appreciated.

The second condition must have a negative impact. For some children not being allowed to join the football game at lunchtime is no disadvantage, they hate kicking footballs around! For some children being alone with their thoughts is not being alone, but is respite from the claustrophobia of a classroom. We are all different and it is important not to assume a negative feeling because you would feel negative in that situation!

We are all different.

The third condition is about protecting the authority of someone to perform a task. Take for example a dentist to whom the child goes because they have a toothache. The dentist says the tooth has to come out and the child says that is unwanted and unwelcome, the pain will have a negative impact and thus the dentist's task constitutes bullying. Here it is clear that if there is a tooth needs extracting it is a warranted action.

Let us now put that situation into a school setting. A student has not completed their homework on the last three occasions. The teacher says that the consequence for this (in line with school policy) is to have a detention (not that detentions necessarily make children do their homework – but let us leave that argument for another time). The child says that this is unwanted treatment, the detention will have a negative impact and thus the teacher is bullying them!

Clearly there has to be some way in which sanctions can be applied without the threat of a complaint of 'bullying'.

On the other hand of course the teacher has different ways of exacting the detention:

> 'Chris, you have not done your homework now on three occasions, and you have not given me any reason for not doing it. You know the consequences. Please report to the Detention Room at 3.30 this afternoon.'

Or:

> 'Chris, you make me so cross. You are a contrary student who does their best to annoy people. I hear in the staffroom that I am not the only teacher for whom you do not do homework. Well I am sick to death of it. You are extremely lazy, you have let down this class; everyone else has done their homework – so I am surprised that you think you don't have to. Go to the Detention Room at 3.30 this afternoon!'

As you can see one way would be unwelcome, unwanted, would have a negative impact and be unwarranted.

READING THE SIGNS: HOW TO SPOT BULLYING

Because children can keep quiet about bullying, there are signs which parents/teachers should look for.

Children who are bullied become unhappy and frightened. They don't want to go to school; they walk around the school by themselves, sit in corners, go to the library or find a place where the bullies are unable to bully them. They don't have friends and they don't want to invite other children home.

Some children become physically ill, saying that they have headaches, tummy aches and feel sick. Whilst these may be psychosomatic, they are real enough for the child. The young person does feel ill, anxiety does cause the head to ache and upset stomachs and irritable bowel syndrome may be consequences of tension or fear of what might happen at school the next day.

They might lie and tell their parents/carers that school is closed for a teacher-only day.

They may also be having nightmares, brought on by being chased, or by the threat of being punched, thumped or jostled. Sleepless nights or those beset with sleep disturbances render the child tired, listless and worn out. They stop running and jumping, skipping and singing. Their eyes become dull and unseeing.

They don't want to talk about school, they become more and more silent and more and more withdrawn. Parents might think back to how their child was behaving a month ago, a term ago, a year ago, at their former school. Have they changed? How?

Some other indicators are:

- frequently lost school equipment, clothing or other personal possessions
- pencil cases and books scrawled over
- unexplained crying at night, especially on Sunday evenings
- fear of starting the new term
- frequent sore throats, headaches, tummy aches and other illnesses
- bedwetting
- nightmares

- anonymous phone calls/fear of picking up texts, voicemails or emails.

WHY ARE CERTAIN CHILDREN TARGETED?

As the stories in this book demonstrate, bullying can take many forms and can affect children in many different ways. The data from exit interviews from school leavers found that 87 per cent of children experience some sort of bullying during their school career. Most deal with it appropriately, learn to walk away, defuse it or ignore it. There will always be people who are sarcastic, who put people down, who make others uncomfortable, who criticize, compare and generally cause grief to their peers, their subordinates or people who are weaker than they are.

So if most children are targets of bullying, why do some children feel it so badly? For these children it is often the case that there are a series of difficult situations happening at the same time. Struggling with academic work, changing schools, having a baby born in the house, parents arguing, parents divorcing, a parent made redundant, moving house, a grandparent very ill or dying, an older brother engaged in drugs or alcohol abuse. These situations make a child's life insecure, unstable and unpredictable. Bullying behaviour that undermines their last shreds of confidence can be the straw that breaks the camel's back and results in a child feeling the bullying much more acutely than others.

However, it would also be naïve to ignore the fact that some children attract bullying. They can make themselves targets by their desperation to be accepted by their peers or by being just plain maddening in the way they behave (often having no 'shut off valve', expressing an opinion at every turn and never learning to keep quiet and listen to others).

While, as an adult, one can understand and perhaps put up with the irritation of these children and be tolerant, the irritation felt by other children must not be allowed to develop into bullying – yet it can be so easy! Watching four children playing football in a cooperative way, sharing the ball and taking turns in the goal is very satisfactory. Then a fifth child turns up and asks to play. The children make allowances, change the rules to accommodate the extra person to find that this child runs off with the ball and hides it. After a few such experiences the four children gang together and tell the fifth child to 'Go away. We don't want you playing with us' – and the fifth child reports back to their teacher that they have been 'bullied'.

Bullying can also happen in the home by older brothers and sisters. Sustained bullying by adult family members and extended family members such as grandparents and cousins is not unusual either. Teachers can also mete out bullying as some of the stories in this book illustrate. This is inexcusable behaviour.

Some children become targets for less obvious reasons:

- Body language – hanging the head, hunching the shoulders, lack of eye contact: expressions of the desire to be invisible. These children can't or won't fight back so they are safe targets.
- Being too clever/too slow.
- Being too fat/thin/plain/tall/short.
- Being too pretty (jealousy of other girls can lead to bullying).
- Being a loner.
- Being no good at sport.
- Wearing spectacles.
- Being different in any way – in dress/sexual preference/ colour/background.

All of the above give opportunities for bullying, particularly if the child targeted is not articulate, has no friends and if the person doing the bullying has an admiration society to support/back up/provoke.

If children are self-confident and secure – and this self-confidence often comes from knowing that they have the unconditional love of their parents or carers – then there is every chance that, even if they are seen to be different in some way, they will be equipped to stand up to peer bullying and become accepted and even admired. If they are not, and they react to taunts and are obviously affected by them, the bullying will continue and, more importantly, have an impact.

WHAT FORMS CAN BULLYING TAKE?

Bullying takes many forms:

- Name-calling and other unwanted verbal abuse.
- Being shouted at.
- Ostracizing a class member and leaving them out of games.
- Unwanted physical contact (hitting/poking/dead arm).
- Spreading of gossip and lies about a child.
- Hiding or destroying belongings.
- Cyber-bullying, such as sending threatening emails, MSN and text messages and other uses of the internet and mobile phones for bullying.
- Unkind, harsh comments by teachers aimed at one child to humiliate him or her in front of others.
- Racial taunts/comments.
- Staring at someone (evil eyes/ dead eyes).
- Gestures which are intimidating, sexual, racial, homophobic or cultural.
- Gang intimidation (waiting, watching, following, stalking).
- Writing (notes or poems, scrawling on belongings, graffiti on blackboards, in toilets and other public places).

Cyber-bullying, such as sending threatening emails, MSN and text messages...

WHO DOES THE BULLYING?

Anyone can use bullying behaviour – anyone can be the victim or target of unwanted, unpleasant bullying treatment. It doesn't matter how old or how young you are.

At Red Balloon we are very keen that children or young people are not labelled 'bullies' and thus throughout this book we do not use that term; rather we use the phrase 'children who use bullying behaviour'. This is for one simple reason. By calling a person a 'bully' we are defining that person's character, behaviour, personality and lifestyle choice. It's a bit like being English, American or Dutch. That is what you are and it implies that there can be no change. I didn't choose to be English – and even if I didn't want to be I can't alter the fact.

But bullying isn't like that. I can choose whether I use bullying behaviour or not. I may have learned to use this unpleasant form of behaviour, but with help, or determination, I could change from using bullying tactics to being kinder, more conciliatory or more understanding.

Bullying is about controlling others and the abuse of power. Power comes in many forms. It is not the same as strength. Size and age don't count for everything. Youngsters who use bullying behaviour can be smaller than their victims, and they can be younger, too. They might be cleverer than the victim or more devious or less constrained by people's opinions. She or he might be in a gang, be a member of the in-group, be the teacher's pet, or think they are the prettiest or the most macho, or the wealthiest.

Children who bully come from all sorts of homes, but one thing is clear – the child who bullies is not a happy child and is probably being bullied by someone else with more power than they have, such as a parent or an older sibling.

Adults such as teachers, neighbours, and grandparents can use bullying tactics and use threatening behaviour towards children. Children and young people can use bullying behaviour towards teachers, neighbours and grandparents too. Bullying behaviour does not just happen within the school gates.

People who bully can act alone, in a small group of two or three, or in a gang.

Lone bullying

Less usual than 'gang bullying', the lone person who uses bullying is often an insecure child who spots one more vulnerable than them and sees a way to control the victim.

Bullying by small groups or gangs

Gang bullying is much more common. Children in a pack can be deadly, encouraging one another to mete out ever more frightening forms of bullying to their unfortunate victim. Usually initiated by a gang leader who gets a kick out of the discomfort of others they have the ability to gather acolytes around him or her and torment others. Joining such a gang can insulate members from being targeted themselves and is a form of security for weak children who will do anything to gain the respect of the gang leader and of their peers. Gang leaders are often deeply unhappy young people who only target others because of their own lack of self-esteem.

WHY DO BULLIED CHILDREN REMAIN SILENT?

Children are often frightened to tell adults they are being bullied. There are many reasons why children put up with their bullying rather than tell. Here are some of them.

They may be frightened:

- that the bullying will get worse
- that they will not be believed
- of being seen as a 'cry-baby', a wimp, a weakling
- that they will be blamed for 'asking for it'
- of getting the child who has been bullying them into trouble

- of involving parents in case they get upset or angry
- of not being taken seriously.

They may have feelings that they:

- have asked for it, provoked it in some way
- are guilty of using bullying behaviour too
- are pathetic if they haven't dealt with it
- will be ostracized by other students
- are exaggerating and the person who bullied them didn't really mean it
- are being oversensitive
- deserve it because they are worthless.

They may keep quiet because they don't know:

- what to do
- that the treatment they are receiving is bullying
- who to go to
- that the school takes bullying seriously.

They may keep quiet because they know that:

- it hasn't been dealt with properly before
- it will get worse
- people who complain are disliked
- the child doing the bullying is a popular student
- they are different from the rest
- their parents are very busy and easily stressed.

They may keep quiet hoping:

- that it will go away
- that the child doing the bullying will get bored and stop

- that the child doing the bullying will leave
- that the child doing the bullying will turn his or her attention to someone else.

10

Practical Coping Strategies for Teachers, Parents and Children

Carrie Herbert

WHAT CAN TEACHERS DO?

Time spent getting to know the children in your care will pay dividends in terms of happiness in the classroom and quality learning; unhappy or frightened children are in no frame of mind to learn. Teach them to manage their anger, make friends with one another, deal with conflict and work as a tight community. Education is not only about achieving academic targets. It is crucially important to put emphasis on producing rounded, kind, emotionally intelligent young people.

Teachers will throw up their hands in horror. 'Time! When do we have time to do all that?! We have no time for anything outside the curriculum.'

But introducing more humanity into the classroom need not be particularly time consuming or difficult.

Forty per cent of the time at Red Balloon is spent dealing with personal and social issues. This is centred around 'Knowing me, knowing you'. If children do not engage in empathy, cannot put themselves in other people's shoes or see something from a different perspective how can they possibly understand others' hurt, pain, embarrassment or humiliation?

At Red Balloon, one of the most successful ways of getting children to talk to one another and to air grievances and fears is through the teacher-led Circle Time where the whole group comes together for discussion. In mainstream school this can be during a PSE session or can be assembled more informally when the need arises. Mix children up on these occasions so that they aren't sitting with their special friends.

It is important that teachers involve students as much as possible in countering bullying. Here are some ideas:

- Appoint and train anti-bullying counsellors or peer mediators (a peer group support structure that can deal with incidents of bullying without going through teachers). Peer group support can provide an opportunity to talk through problems without involving parents and help the recipient confront the bullying activity or use assertive techniques.
- Use Circle Time to raise issues of community health and classroom coherence.
- Teach children skills of negotiation, conflict resolution, assertion and listening. Do this through drama and role-play. Use literature to discuss how the characters within it use bullying tactics or survive bullying behaviour.
- Challenge aggressive bullying behaviour by children who use these tactics and point out other ways of behaving. Return to this conversation on more than one occasion.
- Distribute a questionnaire to discover what the children feel/know about bullying in school.
- Use 'Bullying' as a topic to research characters in history such as Henry VIII, Hitler, etc.
- Bullying frequently happens in unsupervised places like toilets, bike sheds and the playground. Ask the students where the 'dangerous places' and the 'safe places' are at school. Discuss with students/colleagues how to monitor these 'danger spots'.

Teachers can model positive roles in terms of communication, attentive listening and showing respect for others:

- Listen to, believe and support children who say they have been bullied.
- Ask children how they want to deal with the incident or how they want the incident dealt with.
- Use non-bullying methods of teaching.
- Teach students about bullying, what it is, why it is detrimental and where recipients can go for help.
- Discuss incidents of bullying, aggressive behaviour or ostracism as they arise.
- Respond immediately and unambiguously to incidents.
- Build positive self-images amongst the students.
- Commend appropriate behaviour.

And here are counter-bullying measures that are already being implemented by some schools. They have:

- helped the students write and implement a whole school anti-bullying policy
- involved parents in implementing it
- had each class agree on certain rules, rights and responsibilities
- started a 'buddy' system
- set up a 'listener' or a peer mediator system
- written a Student Behaviour Policy
- offered quiet study rooms at playtime
- organized clubs and games at lunchtime
- arranged to have parents on duty at going home time
- trained dinner supervisors to help children organize activities at lunchtime
- taught all children to mediate/intervene where they see bullying or go and tell a teacher
- have a teacher named as the person to whom a child goes if they feel they are being bullied
- taught children who use bullying behaviour different ways to behave
- put a parent traveller on the school buses.

Helping children who use bullying behaviour

Bullying is learned behaviour. In other words, children are not born knowing how to bully, so given the right attention and learning environment they can change their behaviour. Unfortunately, many people think that we must frighten these children into not bullying. Punitive treatment towards those who bully can reinforce their view that when they get big/powerful enough they will be able to use bullying tactics again. Education and raising awareness is much more effective.

Treating a child who uses bullying behaviour with respect and dignity, as well as making them understand that their behaviour has been hurtful, is the best way forward.

The child who bullies may be able to offer useful suggestions for improving the situation. If a gang is doing bullying, identify the leader and talk to him or her.

Most children who bully are happy enough to talk about what has happened so long as they think you are being reasonable and empathetic.

When dealing with a child accused of bullying, defuse the situation; do not exacerbate it by being angry, sarcastic or indignant. The goal is to try and get the person who is using bullying behaviour to feel concern for the recipient.

Try to communicate with these students on equal terms, rather than from a hierarchical position and accept their account, initially, to keep them talking.

When challenging a child accused of bullying about their behaviour and working towards a resolution, try the following statements/questions: 'I would like to talk to you because I've heard that Chris has been having a bad time' or 'I need your help. Chris has been rather upset recently. What do you know about all this?' or 'What have you seen?' After you have made the first couple of statements, remain silent and wait for the perpetrator to respond. (This may seem to take forever, but wherever possible don't rescue them by talking to ease the tension.)

Let them tell you their side of the incident, do not interrupt but encourage them to continue.

When you detect a note of concern for the other child, stop the conversation. Reinforce the notion that you both agree that something is wrong with Chris and he/she has been upset. Elicit constructive solutions: 'What shall we do about it?'

Accept their suggestions, if reasonable, and then tell them that you will meet again in a few days to discuss how things have gone. Arrange a time/date/place to meet.

Aim to get the children together for a constructive talk. This may take some time to achieve and is not always advisable. If a buddy system is operating in the school, the presence of the buddies may help.

Helping a child who has been bullied

Ideally, bullying in school should be swiftly identified and dealt with within the institution. However, it may be that the school feels it is also appropriate to liaise with the parents or carers of the child being bullied. Or it may be that parents pick up on it first and approach the child's teacher.

It is important, in the first instance, to believe the child's perception of what happened and to assure them that they have acted correctly in coming to you. Actively listen to them (stop what you are doing, look at them, respond by nodding and making supportive sounds).

Ask them to tell you what happened by asking neutral questions such as:

> 'Tell me what happened.'
>
> 'Who was involved?'
>
> 'When and where did this happen?'
>
> 'What did you say or do at the time?'
>
> 'How often has this happened, or is this the first time?'
>
> 'Have you spoken to anyone else about this incident/these incidents?'
>
> 'How have you been affected by this bullying or harassment?'

It is not helpful to anyone if you conduct an interrogation or if you make comments or ask questions that make them feel that in some way they were responsible for the behaviour, or that their complaint is trivial or time wasting. In other words, do not convey the impression that the child should feel guilty about being bullied and needing to seek help.

Bullied children need support. They need protection in the first instance, but then they need empowering. Children who are bullied often lack self-esteem and have a negative self-image, so it is important to build up their self-confidence as well as giving them good sound practicable strategies to use in the face of ongoing bullying.

One way of empowering children is to ask them what they want to do. Give them options for dealing with the bullying.

There are about seven major ways of dealing with all kinds of bullying. Adjust them to suit each situation.

1. *Wait and see if it happens again.* For some children the bullying behaviour has only happened once. It may not happen again and they do not want to exacerbate the situation by confronting the child who did it. Maybe it was a mistake; maybe the child who said it or did it was not directing their anger towards the child who felt it. Perhaps the 'victim' has got the wrong end of the stick. Whatever has occurred the child who is doing the complaining has the right to do nothing and wait and see.

2. *Ask the person doing the bullying to stop.* Again we are empowering the recipient. But asking the person who has upset them to stop is a difficult task and must be thought about carefully. The ethos and values in a school will play a part here. If children are encouraged to speak up, 'to tell', to ask teachers for help then it is likely to work. If a school calls children who tell 'tell tale tits' then it is unlikely to be successful. However if a child does want to confront the perpetrator here are three things they can say:

    - what, where, when: 'Yesterday in the canteen you called me a sad cow'
    - how they felt and the impact it had – 'I felt insulted and very angry'
    - what they want to happen now – 'I never want you to do that again'.

3. *Write a letter to the person doing the bullying saying what you would have said if you had been able to say it to their face.*

4. *Ask a student witness to help.* If there was someone who saw what happened or what was said, ask them to get involved. They may need some coaching from the teacher, but essentially we are empowering bystanders to take part and stop the bullying behaviour.

5. *Ask a peer mediator to help solve the problem.*

6. *Ask a teacher to mediate.*

7. *Ask to make a formal complaint.*

REACTING TO PARENTS' COMPLAINTS ABOUT BULLYING

Parents whose children have been bullied are very anxious, sometimes angry, sometimes tearful – whichever way they arrive they will be emotional. It is always important to listen to them and to take their complaint or description of what has happened seriously.

Of course there are children who tell their parents one thing and from your perspective there is an alternative viewpoint. One of the children we had at Red Balloon some time ago had been in this predicament. Both the mother and girl herself were clear that she had been subjected to bullying on a daily basis. She was called names, ostracized, played tricks on and generally shunned by every child in the class. In fact on one occasion she was not invited to another child's party, even though the rest of the class were.

I was contacted by the parent who told me of this situation. I knew the head-teacher of the school in question quite well and spoke to him. He felt that the staff needed some help and guidance on 'this bullying business' and asked me to run some workshops for the staff in order to raise their awareness of the problem, give them strategies for dealing with it, help them find ways of empowering the target and changing the behaviour of the child doing the bullying. I saw the staff at least five times during the course of the next term.

The following term the mother of the girl rang me to tell me that the bullying had started again. I rang the head. He said he would look into it. A week later he rang me back. He had watched the girl in question and whenever he had seen her in the corridor, in the lunch queue or arriving or leaving school she had given him a big smile. When he had asked her if everything had been all right that day she had replied 'Yes, thank you, sir'.

The point about this story is that children, like adults, hide their feelings. Just because someone has a grin on their face does not mean that they are happy. Smiling may just be a front. Walking around as though you are about to burst into tears is the worst thing you can do if you feel you are being bullied. So one way of trying to deal with the situation is to try to look happy. To have that misinterpreted by a teacher or a head who makes the assumption – you are smiling therefore you must be happy – is very unhelpful, if understandable.

In this case, despite the head's assurances that the child really was happy, within five months the girl had voted with her feet and stopped attending school. When Red Balloon admitted the girl, she had seriously low self-esteem; we helped her finish her studies and go on to sixth form.

Believing children, at least in the first instance, is essential. Perceptions are different and we do not know what it is like to be a 13-year-old in a class with others giving us a hard time. Remember, 'Don't you have a bathroom in your house because you smell' doesn't have to be repeated. A tap on the side of the nose across a crowded assembly hall, down the lunch queue, in the playground reminds the target what the sender thinks.

So whatever you think is happening and however much you believe the child is making it up, exaggerating or 'asking for it' listen and then ask, 'What do you want me to do about it?' or 'What do you think is the best way forward from here?' Working together to overcome the situation will help both the parent and the child and in due course the rest of the class as well.

WHAT CAN PARENTS DO?

It is often very difficult to know how to respond to a child who is feeling frightened, humiliated and demeaned and whose self-confidence is at a low ebb. But as a parent you have a very important role to play and you are in a good position to help your child get through this particularly distressing and difficult time.

Sometimes your feelings will get bound up with those of your child and you will feel angry and frustrated. This is a natural reaction. It is important to talk about your own feelings as you encourage your child to talk about theirs. Keeping the door open and not getting angry with them will help your child know that at least there is someone on their side.

What not to say

Helping your child talk about bullying is an essential part of recovery. If a child bottles his or her feelings up, they will become more stressed and so more likely to have physical illnesses. Helping children talk about their suffering is not easy. Many children are reluctant to tell an adult what is happening or who is involved. So you must be very sensitive to their feelings and their needs.

Don't say:

> 'Don't be a baby. It's part of being at school.'
>
> 'Look, I was bullied all the time when I was a kid. There's nothing wrong with it. You'll survive!'
>
> 'Just stop moaning about it. It's normal for children to behave like that.'
>
> 'You're such a wimp. Stand up for yourself and give them back what they give you. Teach the bully a lesson.'

None of these approaches will help a child who is scared, miserable, lonely and whose confidence is at rock bottom.

Listen to your child, let them describe to you what is happening to them, believe them and let them know that you are on their side and will do everything you can to help them.

It is important to bring bullying behaviour to the attention of the school. Whilst your child may be reluctant to do anything about it, nothing will be done if what is happening remains shrouded in silence. Those doing the bullying will think that this behaviour is condoned and will never learn new ways of behaving. Also, while the bullying of your child may eventually stop by itself, another child is bound to be picked on. Talk to your child about the good that will come from telling the school, and support them when they do it. You might want to go to the school and talk to someone without your child being present. Here are a few tips:

- Cool down. Don't act in haste.
- Ring the school and ask to make an appointment to speak to the person in charge of bullying/behaviour/pastoral issues. If there is no such teacher, ask to speak to the head of year, your child's class teacher, the deputy head or the head-teacher.
- Go to the meeting prepared with the information that you have from your child and your own thoughts on the matter, such as:
    - the name of the child – or children – doing the bullying
    - when the incident occurred
    - how it has affected your son or daughter
    - what you want to happen.
- Ask what can be done to help this situation. Work together with the school to try and solve this problem. Don't expect miracles, but slow, steady progress.
- At the interview with a member of staff be prepared to hear that your child is no angel! Try not to get defensive. Some incidents of bullying are started by a child who is using inappropriate behaviour, like barging in on games or taking a group's ball.
- Try together to work out some strategies that can be used immediately – strategies that you can use at home and strategies that the school will use. (See 'What can children do?' for further coping strategies, pp.166–169.)

- One of the things you may be asking for is protection for your child. Work out with the teacher how this will be achieved. For example, if the bullying is happening at break and lunchtime you may decide that staying in would better protect your child. Could the school library or the computer room be used for this purpose? If the bullying happens on the bus home, is it possible to put an adult on the bus for a few weeks until a more permanent solution can be found?
- Remember, you have every right to ask that your son or daughter be treated with respect and dignity at school and that they learn in a safe environment.

Asking the enemy in!

If your son or daughter has a best friend, or a group of best friends, tiffs and arguments are inevitable. Sometimes when splits occur in friendship groups, children find new friends, move on and everything is all right.

Sometimes this is not the case, and some of the group gang up against one 'friend' and bully him or her. It may be possible to break this cycle by inviting one of these children into your own home.

Ask your son or daughter if they would like to try to mend the friendship in this way. Have a meal, talk generally about friendships, make it clear to your guest that they are valued and their company is welcome, and then give the children some space to make up.

Intervention

If a child who has never been a friend is bullying your child, there may be a case for both sets of parents getting together to see if they can sort out the problem cooperatively.

Ask your child who is making them frightened or hitting or humiliating them and contact his or her parents. They may be totally unaware that their child has been involved in bullying. Don't go in all guns blazing! Don't accuse their child of being a bully. This will not help. Instead, talk about the behaviour which is causing distress to your son or daughter. Behaviour can be changed with some reflection, thought and practice. See if you can arrange to meet. Discuss the problem as adults trying to sort out a problem, not as 'us' against 'them'.

Changing schools – a cop-out or just making a sensible choice?

Your child is unhappy, scared, lonely and hates their school. It may have crossed your mind to move them to another school in your area. Don't dismiss it as a negative way of solving a problem. You can encourage them to make a sensible choice. You won't be encouraging your child to run away from difficult situations. There are some problems that are too big to deal with and some that are not worth fighting. Your child's case may be one of these and your energies might be better used elsewhere.

While it is important to stand up to the child or children doing the bullying, there might come a time when to do so becomes destructive. For instance, the school might be unhelpful, the tactics that have been tried might have made the situation worse, the aggressor/s might become more hostile or dangerous. A positive option is to remove your child from the problem.

Think through the alternatives, discuss the possibilities with your child and work out the pros and cons. It is perfectly reasonable to move your child to a school where they can be happy, they will not be bullied and they can learn in peace. It does not follow that because they were bullied at one school they will be bullied at another. However, it is important to arrange the move to another school before your son's or daughter's self-esteem is so low that they 'see' bullying in every glance, giggle and whispered conversation.

So if you think a move away from a gang of bullies might be the answer make an appointment and go together with your child to visit the prospective new school. Ask about their bullying policy. Ask them what they can do to help your child settle in positively. Be honest about the problems you have had. The school will be more able to deal with potential bullying if they know what has gone on before.

WHAT CAN CHILDREN DO?

Some ways of reacting to bullying

Before it happens:

- Avoid certain areas of the school.
- Avoid certain people.
- Ask friends to stay with you before you go into a 'dangerous' area.
- Tell your parents or a trusted friend what frightens you.
- Practise saying 'no'.
- Say out loud the names they are calling you. Say them to a mirror. Try to make them sound normal and not hurtful.
- Practise looking happy and unconcerned.

At the time:

- Ask the child/children doing the bullying to stop that particular behaviour.
- Walk away.
- Ignore it and think positive thoughts.
- Find your friends (or another group of people) and stay with them.
- Make a joke about it.

After it has happened:

- Tell a teacher.
- Find your friends and tell them what has happened.
- Tell your parents.

There are some simple techniques you can learn, but not all of them are suitable for all situations and one of the most difficult things is to work out which one is best for which situation.

WALKING AWAY

Teach yourself to walk away from a situation in which you feel unsafe or threatened. Keep your shoulders back and your head up and, with the child or children doing the bullying still in your sight, walk away – sideways, if necessary, if you think it may be dangerous to turn your back on a crowd.

POSITIVE SELF-TALK

Positive self-talk is a way of keeping calm in a difficult and negative situation. If you think one or more children may subject you to nasty and unkind remarks, try thinking beforehand about the things you are good at. Write them down and when you are being called names, think of this list and repeat it silently in your head. For instance, you might say things like:

> 'I'm good at art, I love my family and my pets and they love me. Lucy likes me and I'm her best friend. I like her mum and dad and they like me. My Gran loves me, Auntie Jo loves me and I love playing with my cousins.'

SAYING 'NO'

Be assertive when you don't want to do something/want something to happen. Start a sentence with a clear 'No' before stating what you don't want. For example:

> 'No, I don't want to go to the playing field.'
>
> 'No, I won't lend you my bike.'

FOGGING

Fogging is a way of deflecting unkind or cruel statements. You accept what is said, agree with it and move on. For instance, if someone was to say to you, 'You've got a big bum', you could reply with, 'Yes, I have, haven't I.' This technique can be used to reply to all nasty taunts whether it is to do with glasses, your weight, your height, your hair or your clothes. But practise it. Remembering to say these things calmly in a stressful situation is easier if you have tried them out before – even if just in the mirror!

BROKEN RECORD

Look the person doing the bullying in the eye and repeat the same statement over and over again so that you don't get caught up in silly arguments. For example, say the person bullying you tries to stop you leaving the school gates. He/she is standing there and may try to involve you in a quarrel which could lead to a fight. Don't get drawn in. Keep repeating a polite, neutral statement such as 'I must go home. I would like to get past please.'

ENLISTING SUPPORT

If there are certain times in the school day when you are being bullied you could try to ask someone to help you get through them. For example, if the bullying happens at lunchtime, try asking a friend to come with you, to sit with you at the table, to stand near you in the playground. If you are being bullied as you collect your bike, ask someone to come with you to the bike shed. It could be an older student or a friend.

USING ASSERTIVE BEHAVIOUR

As well as using assertive words (saying 'No') use assertive body language. Standing up tall, keeping your shoulders back, your head up and looking the person in the eye will give a strong message in itself. Try to look calm even if you are feeling scared inside. Take deep breaths to give your body plenty of oxygen. Your brain can think better if you have a good supply of oxygen. Your voice will work better too.

TRICKING

Using devious methods to protect oneself should only be used in dangerous situations. For example, if you are surrounded by a gang who intend to do you some harm, shouting 'That's my older sister' or

'There's my father' may get you out of that situation. *This is a short-term solution only.*

SELF-ESTEEM

Often people who are bullied feel bad about themselves and say things like, 'I really deserve to be bullied because I'm not a very nice person.' These feelings are because you have low self-esteem. It is quite difficult to raise your self-esteem, but it is important you try to do it. Think about the things you like doing, the things you are good at, the things that make you happy and positive about yourself. Write them down in a private book. Write down nice things that other people say to you. Keep letters and cards which people send you and which often have kind thoughts and writings inside them – for example, 'To my special niece' or 'To my beautiful Granddaughter'. When you are feeling low, take them out and re-read them.

SEEKING HELP

If you are suffering from being bullied, *you must tell someone.* If you are frightened of confiding in your teachers or your parents, there are other people who can help you. A neighbour, your doctor, the nurse at school, a friend's parents, an aunt or uncle, grandparents, an older brother or sister. A problem shared is a problem halved and, *however bad the situation,* there is *always* a solution.

FROM DESPAIR TO RECOVERY

Moving on

Finally, to bring home what these approaches mean in practice, here are some of the many messages Red Balloon has received from parents and ex-students who have benefited from these approaches.

They provide a very real reminder of the crippling effect bullying has on the lives of the children who experience it, and also their families, and offer a powerful case for all of us to remain vigilant to the seriousness of bullying and to take measures where we can to address it in our daily work in caring for children.

LETTERS FROM PARENTS

'My son was severely bullied during the two years he spent at our local community college.

Every day he was hit, pushed, kicked and called names. He was also spat on. I remember telling the head-teacher that his uniform was covered in other people's spit most days. I had many conversations with staff at the school about the bullying and our son's poor attendance. He was admitted to hospital because the stomach pains he was suffering were so severe that his consultant suspected an ulcer. Eventually I was told that his pain was very real but it was 'psychological in origin'. He also suffered from the most appalling migraines and was prescribed medication for these.

My happy son completely disappeared. He became clinically depressed and started to self-harm. He started to overdose on medication in an attempt to make himself too sick to attend school. I began to think I might lose him. I continued to visit his school, but the situation didn't improve and the bullying didn't stop.

During this time I was absolutely desperate for help. I had no one to turn to and I didn't know what to do. Even though I've lived in Cambridge for 20 years, I'd never heard of Red Balloon. Then one day I typed 'Help, bullied Cambridge' into my computer and the Red Balloon popped up. I phoned the school and Carrie Herbert happened to answer the phone. During that conversation she made me feel like I wasn't going mad and there was hope for my son. I had found someone who wanted to help us.

I haven't got the words to express how significant Red Balloon has been in the life of my son and his family. He now has an excellent attendance record, doesn't suffer from stomach pain or migraine, is receiving a first-class education but, more than any of that, he's not afraid of everything anymore. He's started to trust his peer group and sometimes he even seems happy!

I can't imagine what would have happened to my son without Red Balloon. Actually, I can imagine it, and I feel totally blessed that we found Red Balloon.

In my opinion Red Balloon has quite possibly saved my son and given him the opportunity to lead a normal and productive life.

The Red Balloon staff have provided an environment that is free of the fear and misery that used to dominate his experience of school, they have tried to give him a sense of his own worth and they have filled his life with love and support.'

'I've been meaning to write this for ages to tell you how [our child] is getting on.

Over the last two or three months, things have gradually improved. By the end of last term, she was in most days. She is starting to make a couple of friends and although she is far from confident, she is getting into most classes. She is still quite good at avoiding doing school work, but has sat her first GCSE module exams in science and maths. I didn't even expect her to be able to go into the exam room, but she revised hard for both for about two weeks and got an A* in the science. She will get the maths result next term.

Thanks again for all you did for her and for the support you gave me.'

'[Our child] had an absolutely wonderful time last week, and I just want to thank you for everything. The train trip, the actual venue, the chef, everything must have taken quite some organizing. But what a success! What a great place, he loved the beauty, the views, the food – everything. What's more, I even managed not to phone to check how he was getting on!

He has come back with a new sense of himself, a new confidence, and a realization that he is able to be and do so much more than he had realized. In fact this is something that is constantly changing at the moment – his perception of himself.

He also loved having the time to get to know everybody there better. Thanks for letting them chat late on their last night! The fun, the nonsense, the camaraderie and the 'bonding' are all so much more important than sleep! Thanks for encouraging the 'hero' in him to climb that mountain even while he felt so unwell. He has learned priceless lessons during his week away, and you all feature greatly in our evening conversations at the moment!

We are so proud of him, and so grateful to you all for having such faith in our wonderful son, and for creating an environment where he can flourish and grow and learn to be proud of himself. (He is apparently quite awesome, so he keeps telling us, which is nice.)'

MESSAGES FROM EX-STUDENTS

'I have enjoyed my time here immensely and look forward to the months ahead and the unpredictability of the passing days. I have made brilliant acquaintances with everyone at the Red Balloon Norwich and have made good friends with others. Everyone here has an amazing ability to not only have fun but to care for one another. I have had a difficult time at home and at school, but have found that honesty is the best policy. I have worked hard in all lessons and have tried my utmost to complete my work correctly.

Singing and cooking lessons with Maria have been very beneficial. My basic cooking skills have improved and I have used some of the recipes at home, which everyone has enjoyed tasting. My vocal range has expanded, my confidence has grown and my ability and strength have spiralled. Art and design lessons with Alex have been difficult for me. We have now resolved our differences and now I really enjoy my lessons with her. My project is steaming ahead and I cannot wait to complete it. English language has been full on but my great connection with Mary has made my lessons enjoyable. Her sense of humour is similar to mine and she reminds me a lot of my mum. I have only had a few lessons with Rosario but all of them have been educational and fun. I have only had one lesson with Sarah senior but have enjoyed her smiles and charm that she always carries. Janet has a special quality to make even the most difficult of work seem easy. I enjoyed my trip to the Red Cross with her. Her Tesco's red beret and French air made it feel as if we were in the streets of France. My maths lessons with Jenny have been hard work but I have learned much from our time together and will enjoy many lessons to come. Richard is an absolute gentleman and has made me laugh on many occasions. Pat is a woman with a beautiful heart and together with Richard I see them as the mum and dad of our small community. Jean has been very supportive and has helped many people at the Red Balloon. The wonderful people who run music workshops with us make Friday afternoons enjoyable and I always look forward to my time with them. I have not seen much of Louise as she is a very hard worker, but she cares a lot for everyone and helps out when she can. Ruth and Carrie are amazing people and without them I would not be here now. The students here are more than understanding about each other's needs and problems. I cannot wait until the rest of the year ahead and want to thank all the volunteers for their time.'

'I've thought about writing this letter several times but never known where to start. My reason for writing is that I've reached a point in my life where I am achieving my goals and I am genuinely happy. I still have my ups and downs but I'm out in the world and living the life I want to. I thought I'd write now that I have reached this point to provide hope to any students who may be feeling as scared, lonely, low and unhappy as I once did. Although it might not feel like it now, there *is* a way out of it and when you find it you, too, will go on to achieve your goals. My message to other students would be believe in yourself, trust your instincts and everything else will fall into place.'

I fit in, I have friends, I'm not behind in class and I'm not the stupid one that needs help. I'm the one that has all the answers! I'm a bit of a geek! I thought I would go back to the role of being the shy girl that everyone thinks is a freak and not cope with the work. I thought it would be like when I was a child. But I'm not and I *never* will be that girl again. I *can* do the work! I'm not stupid, and I know it!

I feel like I've got a bit of my childhood back. I was always so jealous of the kids that had the experience of going to school and it being fun because they had friends and boys to fancy and nothing holding them back and they could do the work, and nobody thinks you're a freak. I guess this is the closest I'll ever get to being a 'normal' kid in school having fun. But we all know I'll never be normal – I'm too special to be normal!'

'Red Balloon made me feel human and made me feel safe and made me feel that I matter.

When everything was going on at my other school I felt less than human, like an animal or a lesser being. I wanted to commit suicide and if it wasn't for RB I wouldn't be here now. [At Red Balloon] how I felt was important and what I needed was important, and I had time off at the studio if I needed that. It's an amazing place, and it made me feel alive.'

'I loved school. It was the best way to spend my time and I had so much fun. I was set to do 11 GCSEs, all A–B predicted grades, but of course nothing good can last for ever. There are some very spiteful and selfish people out there who choose to ruin life for the rest of us. Have you ever felt so terrified that your body went rigid? I have. That if you try to face something, your mind and body just shut down and you feel like death? I have. Every day for a whole year. Every time I was dropped off at school… I just froze. I couldn't physically make myself move no matter how much I knew I had to. I as good as dropped out of school, my whole life down the pan. No school, no friends, no one to talk to, and no one could get me out of it. I spent months on end at home, and you know the biggest downer of it all? I wanted to learn. I wanted to go back! I just couldn't. You keep trying to find a way out and then you hit a brick wall.

Now I know there are other kids like me, kids who want to learn but can't face mainstream school. We wanted to learn and we got that opportunity to get our lives back; at Red Balloon I got that back.

Have you ever watched your life fall apart and never thought you'd get it back? I have. Have you ever got it back? I have.'

APPENDIX

How Red Balloon Learner Centres Work

Carrie Herbert

PHILOSOPHY

Right from the start, the Red Balloon's philosophy has been to listen to, to teach and to build up the self-esteem of our students.

Being without friends is miserable, being targeted and taunted is miserable and in these circumstances, no one can learn effectively. Also, for whatever reason, some children find learning – and concentration – hard, especially in the classroom. And if they are teased for this, the problem is exacerbated. Tom puts it so well in his story: 'My head would go numb and the words would swim in front of my eyes – so a lot of the time in lessons I'd sort of switch off and think of other things.' And Jane's ordeal, too, will be familiar to many children; here is a child who found reading out loud a real trial, yet she was put on the spot by an insensitive teacher and mocked when she stumbled over her words.

If children have a negative learning experience, see lessons only as something to be endured rather than enjoyed, are led to believe that they are stupid, then they will cease to try, their self-worth will erode and they will either become disruptive or they will turn in on themselves and try to become invisible.

But, given the right conditions, children are eager to learn. They are naturally curious and if they really want to know about something they will pursue the subject with patience and enthusiasm.

At Red Balloon we nurture this enthusiasm, curiosity and patience in every way we can. We give each child individual attention and seek always to find something (a topic, a musical instrument, a sport, art, sewing, dancing, whatever) that engages and enthuses that child and from this starting point we try to build up their confidence and reignite their enjoyment in the learning process.

These, then, are the three main tenets of our philosophy:

Academic achievement

As well as helping each child to work towards his or her potential (at their own pace) and take pride in their achievements, at Red Balloon we have a unique attitude towards failure. Every child coming to a Red Balloon Learner Centre has different educational needs (see 'Negotiating the Curriculum', pp.183–185) and different talents and all of the children who come to us have had a bad time at school. Most think that they have failed in some way, failed themselves, failed to make friends, failed their parents, failed to learn.

At some time or another, we have all experienced a sense of failure. Failure is the most paralysing feeling, so at Red Balloon we do not treat mistakes as failures but as opportunities for the children to re-assess what they need to do to put these mistakes right – and the process of putting them right we treat as achievement. Whether it is something they are making that has gone wrong, some writing that needs attention, a relationship that has turned sour or a sum that needs reworking, Red Balloon staff work with the children and offer them the opportunity to revisit these mistakes in a supportive and positive light.

Listening and discussion

How many of us, when we were young, harboured resentment because we had not been listened to? We may have had a perfectly logical explanation for doing what we did, but we were never given a chance to explain and were punished by adults who couldn't see the world as we saw it. How unfair was that?!

At Red Balloon we believe that time should be made for children and young people to have the chance to speak about their actions in a calm and non-judgemental atmosphere and to explain their reasons for doing what they have done. Children make sense of the world in all sorts of different ways, informed always by the experiences they have had. Their opinions should be given respect and they should be listened to and engaged in discussion. This is dealt with in more depth below (see 'A therapeutic community').

A positive self-image

The children who come to us have low self-esteem and it is essential that this is built up so that they can move on, so we teach social and communication skills at Red Balloon as well as always stressing the positive, whether by praising a piece of work well done, a kindness shown to another student or to a member of staff, a skill learned (such as being able to stand up straight and look someone in the eye). (See 'Personal and Social Education' on p.180.)

A THERAPEUTIC COMMUNITY

At Red Balloon, respect and consideration for each other is paramount, as set out in the conditions of entry to a Red Balloon Learner Centre. Staff show respect and consideration to students and each other, students are expected to show respect and consideration to staff members and to each other.

Our students will react to the traumatic experiences they have been through in various ways – some by yelling and losing their temper, some by bottling up their feelings. Staff at Red Balloon are trained to help the children understand why they feel as they do and teach them to behave more appropriately.

First they need to understand that rude, aggressive, disrespectful or inconsiderate behaviour is not acceptable and, crucially, to realize that when they behave in this way they are upsetting others. They have to learn that *everyone* has feelings. Once a child has recognized that their behaviour is upsetting, then they can go forward and begin to change it.

This won't happen overnight but it is their willingness to try to change, and know that change is necessary, which is important. If they are engaged in the process, then their behaviour will gradually improve.

The children we have at Red Balloon have been ridiculed, humiliated and let down. They have no self-esteem and trust neither themselves nor other people.

At Red Balloon our main aim is to restore children's trust in *themselves*. They are the only ones who ultimately can take responsibility for their own behaviour, so they must begin to learn how to take control of a situation. They need to trust themselves enough to walk away, challenge, apologize, argue or stay silent. They need to have a range of skills in their repertoire so that when faced with a difficult situation they can:

- trust their own reading of it
- trust that they can control their own behaviour
- judge how to behave.

We do not tolerate shouting, raised voices, sarcasm, putdowns, or jokes at another's expense. Some of our children are autistic and take everything literally – and all of our children carry 'baggage'. To say 'I was only joking' in no way excuses a hurtful remark.

This, then, is how our therapeutic community at Red Balloon has evolved, by engendering mutual respect and consideration, by getting students to understand why some behaviour is inappropriate and needs changing, by teaching them the skills necessary to change it and also equipping them with enough self-belief to be able to cope in a challenging situation.

PERSONAL AND SOCIAL EDUCATION

At Red Balloon, a large percentage of our time is devoted to pastoral issues.

Many of our students find communication difficult. They may not be able to look a person in the eye, smile as they speak or make conversation. Some find it hard to know how to respond to their own or others' emotions.

Often this lack of communication skills has led to a child being bullied so we spend time helping students build up these skills in dedicated sessions. Also, during break and lunchtimes there are often opportunities for discussing the results of inappropriate behaviour and giving guidance on an alternative course of action.

Constant supervision during break times is also a priority. Staff are constantly on the lookout for inappropriate behaviour and challenge children if they say something too personal, unkind or as a putdown. Tackling this behaviour quickly and at source is crucial. Equally, if a child is sitting alone at break or lunchtime, they must be sat with; initially a staff member will do this, but later staff may manipulate the situation so that another student sits with this child. However, if a child is more comfortable, at first, as an onlooker, then this should be respected, once checked out.

At Red Balloon, students are not allowed to go outside and 'play' during breaks without a staff member as this may lead to a re-creation of the very situations in which so many students were bullied. So staff make a point of engaging children in conversations during break times, helping them to acquire some of the social skills they lack.

Flexibility is very important at Red Balloon. If, at any time, a child is unhappy or stressed and needs comforting or counselling, then this is available to them. They have ongoing access to various people on the staff or elsewhere in addition to their subject teachers, including:

- student support assistants
- therapists (drama, play, art, cognitive behaviour, music, talk)
- counselling centre
- academic tutor.

And there are also sessions in which pastoral issues are explored:

- drama (1 hour a week)
- Circle Time (1 hour a week)
- boys' group (1 hour a week)
- girls' group (1 hour a week)
- ethics (1 hour a week) – discussion of social issues
- workshops on countering bullying (as required)
- personal and social skills: individual work on self-esteem (as required).

Therapists

At Red Balloon therapists are integrated into the Centre as staff members but it is vital that all the adults at the Centre – not just therapists – know the relevant information about a child so that they can help each student recover effectively. At staff meetings there is frank discussion among teachers about a child's progress, regress, development or about a specific incident or achievement. Therapists are encouraged to shed light from their perspective on a child's personal, social and emotional development.

Before they come to Red Balloon, many students are withdrawn at home. Many are depressed, some self-harm and nearly all of them think that they are to blame for the predicament they are in. Some of these children have not been out of their house for weeks, scared that the 'bullies' will get them. Therapy can help lift the burden of blame and encourage the child to understand in greater depth what happened to them at school.

Working alongside the teaching staff, therapists can enhance the recovery of each child and advise teachers on some counselling strategies. Equally, teachers can usefully describe to the therapist what excites a student in their learning.

Red Balloon also offers Family Therapy.

Drama and ethics

These sessions encourage students to think creatively, to speak out and to see things from other people's viewpoint. In ethics we talk about tricky moral and ethical issues such as animal rights, race, other cultures, euthanasia and drug use. These discussions can be in pairs, small groups, whole groups or take the form of a structured formal debate.

In drama we look at characters within pieces, using improvisation as well as acting out social dramas and current news stories. In the past, for instance, students have acted out aspects of the Madrid train disaster and explored the background of a 13-year-old boy who was convicted of stealing a car, speeding and being drunk. In this scenario, students improvised being the boy's head-teacher, the sister who looked after him, his 'industrious' parents who worked all night, and the staff and other eaters in a fast food restaurant in which he and his mates created havoc. Through this social situation the students worked on a fight scene, involving close physical contact and cooperation, race issues (the meanings of racial harassment and racism were discussed) and they were encouraged to use the range of emotions of anger, fear, sadness and happiness when they acted out their characters.

Boys' and girls' groups

In these single-sex sessions, the students welcome the opportunity to discuss personal and sexual issues without inhibition. They are encouraged to consider how as a girl or a boy they contribute to Red Balloon and whether there are aspects of being a boy or a girl that they would like to challenge. The girls, for instance, often discuss how they can get the boys to be less aggressive, less noisy and more sensitive. A response to this has been to suggest to the girls that they are more assertive, and find ways to challenge the boys' individual behaviour appropriately.

The boys, on the other hand, usually want to talk about sex and girls and this gives an opportunity for discussion about emotions and managing anger. Relationships are often discussed and the boys are encouraged to talk about their feelings and to think about the body language and feelings of others. They are also taught how to recognize anger in themselves and others and deal with it appropriately.

Individual work on self-esteem and facing demons

This takes the form of one to one discussions and small-group tasks designed to help individual students work on particular aspects of their behaviour. Here are two contrasting examples:

1. One girl was very anxious about going outside and had had little experience of shopping so opportunities to go out, in company, and face up to her anxiety were built into her timetable.
2. Another child frequently lost his temper when criticized. Once he had calmed down, a one to one meeting was arranged to address the issue head on. The staff member returned to the particular situation which had so enraged him, discussed his reaction and asked him how he felt when criticized. Then the student was asked some questions. Was the criticism valid? Did he respect the person making the criticism? Was this person an expert, in a position to know better than him? Was his response appropriate and, if not, how should he react in future?

In this way issues and problems can be tackled in a calm and non-confrontational manner, always giving the student respect and affording them the opportunity to find alternatives to their knee-jerk response to situations and giving them time to practise using them in a safe environment.

NEGOTIATING THE CURRICULUM

At Red Balloon we have the expertise to tutor students up to 'A' level but our aim is always to recover them sufficiently so that they can go back into mainstream education as soon as possible.

The needs and interests of the student are our first priority but our philosophy is to place the *responsibility* for learning on the shoulders of the learner, while, at the same time, making every effort to ensure that he or she is stimulated by the learning process.

Every child who comes to Red Balloon has different educational needs. Many have fallen behind in their work because of being out of school for a long period or because they have been so traumatized that they have found it impossible to concentrate in lessons. Others have simply failed to be engaged by conventional methods of teaching and sit in a classroom in an uncomprehending fog. They simply 'don't get it'. Some of these children do get the help they need, but many don't, they begin to feel that they are invisible to the teachers and slip through the net. We all develop at a different rate and in a large class it is difficult to accommodate the needs of every student.

But at Red Balloon this is exactly what we do. Some of our students are very able and once they have the opportunity to study in a safe and non-threatening environment they soon catch up. Others have simply not been engaged at school, have been taunted for being stupid – or for other reasons – their brains have 'frozen' and they have more or less given up on learning.

At Red Balloon, each student learns at their own pace, if appropriate on a one to one basis so that he or she does not have to worry about being shown up in front of their peers.

We always discuss academic expectations with the student and negotiate with them to try and ensure that these are neither too unchallenging nor, indeed, too unrealistic.

It is essential that students are stimulated by what they are doing. In writing a piece, for instance, the children choose their own topic, one about which they are curious, obsessed or excited. Writing is a process, beginning with a period of incubation, thinking about what it is you might write. Who will read the piece, why are you writing the letter, essay, story, review or play? What is the purpose of the writing, what message are you trying to convey? All this helps with clarity, accuracy and meaning.

The author of the piece, not the teacher, decides on the title and plot line. A student then writes, rewrites and asks for feedback. The feedback is specific. Can you tell me if it makes sense? Can you tell me if it sounds spooky enough? The child may of course want a teacher to edit with regard to spelling, grammar or punctuation and here the teacher can teach these skills in context. The inverted commas or speech marks, for instance, are taught when the learner has started to use them in their writing. The rule for 'i' before 'e' except after 'c' is taught when it is required; grammar and punctuation taught out of context can be meaningless to the child.

In this way, the student is given the *time* to produce a well-thought-out, polished piece of work which they 'own' and in which they can take real pride.

The author is always respected and a teacher will neither demolish a piece nor falsely praise it. Comments from a teacher are accepted or rejected by the child as an author would the comments of a critic: to be taken or discarded depending on how much they respect those views. It is their writing not the teacher's.

If there is a formal assessment to be done, children need to know on what basis their piece will be judged. And be part of that process.

Children should never be expected to read out loud without having had the chance to practise. As mentioned before, children at Red Balloon are encouraged to speak publicly every six weeks or so. At the end of each half term every student prepares a talk about a piece of work they are pleased with and this is given in front of the other students and staff. They are helped to prepare for this.

If a teacher is listening to a child reading and they stop, the teacher will say 'Just guess what it might be and keep going.' Interestingly the children normally guess correctly: not necessarily the right word but one that fits the sentence.

Learning is a very private matter; learners should not be watched or looked at but allowed to get on with it on their own. Mistakes should be made in secret, not publicly.

The emphasis of our teaching at Red Balloon is on listening, encouraging, offering choices, challenging and asking meaningful questions. And since we have a flexibility that is impossible to achieve in a mainstream school, we can also create learning opportunities. For instance, if a discussion has stimulated a group of students, then we have the flexibility to build on that interest and extend it into other areas.

This is the learning philosophy on which Red Balloon is based.

USEFUL RESOURCES

Here are some details of various anti-bullying and other charities that are there to offer help, advice and support to children and their families.

UK

Anti-Bullying Alliance

www.anti-bullyingalliance.org.uk
Phone: 020 7843 1901

Beat Bullying

www.beatbullying.org
Email: help@bullying.co.uk
Phone: 0845 3385060
Beat Bullying works with young people to combat bullying and provides information to parents and mentors.

Bully Free Zone

www.bullyfreezone.co.uk
Email: office@bullyfreezone.co.uk
Phone: 01204 454958
They run workshops throughout the North East for people of all ages and offer one to one counseling as well as family support. They have a guide ('Say No to Bullying') and other useful information.

Bullying UK

www.bullying.co.uk
Email: help@bullying.co.uk
This website sets out the many ways in which a child can be bullied (including cyber-bullying) and provides a resource of how and where to get help.

ChildLine

www.childline.org.uk
Helpline: 0800 11 11
Free and confidential advice for children and young adults about a wide range of issues, including bullying.

CyberMentors

www.cybermentors.org.uk
Run by Beat Bullying, CyberMentors mentor and assist other young people who use the website. They have experienced accredited counsellors who are on hand to help.

Each

www.eachaction.org.uk
Helpline: 0808 1000 143 (Monday to Friday, 10am–4pm)
EACH's Actionline takes calls from children and young people (or an adult on their behalf) who are experiencing homophobic bullying anywhere in England and Wales. EACH staff provide professional, confidential support and guidance and can help callers decide on the best course of action. There is now the option to report homophobic bullying online.

Enable Scotland

www.enablemescotland.info
Email: enable@enable.org.uk
Phone: 0141 226 4541
Enable Scotland and respectme (Scotland's Anti-Bullying service) help children and adults with learning disabilities who are affected by bullying.

Get Connected

www.getconnected.org.uk
Helpline: 0808 80 84994
Safe online resource for young people seeking help with personal problems.

Kidscape

www.kidscape.org.uk
Helpline: 08451 205 204
Kidscape offers support and advice to parents of bullied children, literature and videos on bullying, child protection and parenting and offers a training programme on child safety and behaviour management issues. It also provides confidence-building sessions for children who are bullied.

National Bullying Helpline

www.nationalbullyinghelpline.co.uk
Helpline: 0845 225 5787
Gives free support to both adults and children who are experiencing bullying.

NSPCC (National Society for the Prevention of Cruelty to Children)

www.nspcc.org.uk
Helpline: 0808 800 5000
Free and confidential advice for those worried about a child.

Red Balloon Learner Centres

www.redballoonlearner.co.uk
Email: rb@national.redballoonlearner.org.uk
Phone: 01223 366052
This organization helps children who are affected by bullying. It provides education in a safe environment for those who are unable to go to school because they have been severely bullied.

The Place2Be

www.theplace2be.org.uk
Email: enquiries@theplace2be.org.uk
Phone: 020 7923 5500
The Place2Be is a school-based counselling service, dedicated to improving the emotional wellbeing of children, their families and the whole school community.

Think U Know

www.thinkuknow.co.uk
Phone: 0870 000 3344
Guide to internet safety and safe surfing for young people from Think U Know. Think U Know is an education initiative by the Child Exploitation and Online Protection (CEOP) Centre. CEOP is a government-run law enforcement agency and we aim to protect young people from abuse, both online and in the real world.

Australia

Bullying No Way!

www.bullyingnoway.com.au
A website created by Australia's educational communities to create learning environments where every student and school community member is safe from bullying.

Kids Helpline

www.kidshelp.com.au
Helpline: 1800 55 1800
A free 24-hour confidential online and phone counselling service for young people.

USA

Stop Bullying Now!

www.stopbullyingnow.hrsa.gov
US Department of Health and Human Services offering games, movies and information about bullying and how to prevent it.

FURTHER READING

RECOMMENDED READING FOR CHILDREN EXPERIENCING BULLYING

Reading books about bullying often helps children get into perspective what is happening to them. Some children think they are the only ones who are bullied. This makes them feel isolated and different. Reading some stories about bullying will help them understand that this is a problem which other people experience. It also gives them insight into how others felt and coped, and strategies they used to solve the problem. Below is a list of picture books, novels, and non-fiction books.

Fiction for older readers

J. Blume (1974) *Blubber.* Bradbury.
Suggested age range: 9–11

Y. Coppard (1990) *Bully.* Bodley Head.
Suggested age range: 10–15

K. Dicamillo (2001) *Tiger Rising.* Candlewick.
Suggested age range: 10+

C. Forde (2004) *Fat Boy Swim.* Delacorte Press.
Suggested age range: 10+

G. Gardner (2003) *Inventing Elliott.* Orion.
Suggested age range: 10–14

J. Gavin (2004) *Coram Boy.* Egmont.
Suggested age range: 12+

W. Golding (1954) *Lord of the Flies.* Faber & Faber.
Suggested age range: 12+

K. Gray (2003) *Malarkey.* Red Fox.
Suggested age range: 12+

R. Green (2001) *Cuckoos.* Oxford University Press.
Suggested age range: 11+

P. Johnson (2002) *Traitor.* Corgi.
Suggested age range: 10+

P. Johnson (2004) *Avenger.* Yearling, Random House.
Suggested age range: 9+

H. McKay (2003) *Indigo's Star.* Hodder Children's Books.
Suggested age range: 10+

N. Singer (2002) *Feather Boy.* Delacorte Press.
Suggested age range: 9–11

J. Wilson (1996) *Bad Girls.* Corgi.
Suggested age range: 8–11

Fiction for younger children

A. Browne (1985) *Willy the Champ.* Walker Books.
Suggested age range: 6–8

K. Cave (1994) *Something Else.* Viking Children's Books.
Suggested age range: 4–8

A. Durant (2000) *Big Bad Bunny.* Scholastic.
Suggested age range: 5–7

A. Fine (1992) *The Angel of Nitshill Road.* Methuen.
Suggested age range: 7+

V. Ironside (1996) *The Huge Bag of Worries.* Wayland.
Suggested age range: 5–11

D. McKee (1989) *Elmer.* HarperCollins.
Suggested age range: 3+

T. Ross (2004) *Is It Because?* Andersen Press.
Suggested age range: 0–5

F. Simon (1999) *Hugo and the Bully Frogs.* Gullane Children's Books.
Suggested age range: 4–5

J. Wilson (1998) *Monster Eyeballs.* Mammoth.
Suggested age range: 5+

Non-fiction for children and young people

J. Alexander (2003) *Bullies, Big Mouths and So-Called Friends.* Hodder Children's Books.
Suggested age range: 9–12

M. Elliott (1998) *Wise Guides: Bullying.* Hodder Children's Books.
Suggested age range: 10–16

FURTHER READING FOR PARENTS AND PROFESSIONALS

Beane, A. L. (2008) *Protect Your Child from Bullying: Expert Advice to Help you Recognize, Prevent and Stop Bullying Before Your Child Gets Hurt.* San Francisco: Jossey Bass.

Besag, V. (2006) *Understanding Girls' Friendships, Fights and Feuds: A Practical Approach to Girls' Bullying.* Milton Keynes: Open University Press.

Coloroso, B. (2009) *The Bully, the Bullied and the Bystander: From Preschool to Highschool – How Parents and Teachers Can Help Break the Cycle of Violence.* New York: Collins Living.

Haber, J. (2008) *Bullyproof Your Child for Life: Protect Your Child from Teasing, Taunting, and Bullying for Good.* New York: Perigee.

Macintyre, C. (2009) *Bullying and Young Children: Understanding the Issues and Tackling the Problem.* London: Routledge.

Rigby, K. (2007) *Children and Bullying: How Parents and Educators Can Reduce Bullying at School.* Malden, MA: Wiley-Blackwell.

Sullivan, K. (2006) *Bullying: How to Spot It and How to Stop It.* London: Rodale International.

Sullivan, K., Cleary, M. and Sullivan, G. (2003) *Bullying in Secondary Schools: What it Looks Like and How to Manage It.* London: Sage Publications.

Thomson, J. (2005) *Bullying: A Parent's Guide.* Peterborough: Need2Know.